SICKENED

HOW THE GOVERNMENT RUINED HEALTHCARE
AND HOW TO FIX IT

SHAWN NEEDHAM R.PH.

TABLE OF CONTENTS

"It's crazy how many of these stats I am smack in the middle of!"

— **ANONYMOUS READER**

"The investment in educating the patient to be a driver and the hunger so many have to take command of their own Health is real and inspiring."

— **MICHELLE MYERS MURPHY**, ARNP, OWNER OF PEAK PERFORMANCE & PREVENTION, P3LIFE.COM

"History is crystal clear. People pursuing their own self interests in their healthcare decisions tend to be the most healthy."

— **DR. SHANE NEEDHAM**, SCIENTIST / ENTREPRENEUR / TEDX SPEAKER, CO-FOUNDER ALTURAS ANALYTICS

"The federal government is the only health insurance company with tanks and F16's backing it. I felt like an accessory to the crime. So glad I am out of it. Thank you for writing this book."

— **DR KEITH SMITH**, CO-FOUNDER OF THE SURGERY CENTER OF OKLAHOMA AND THE FREE MARKET MEDICAL ASSOCIATION

COPYRIGHT & DISCLOSURES

tices, advertising, and all other aspects of doing business in the US, Canada, or any other jurisdiction is the sole responsibility of the reader or purchaser. Neither the author nor the publisher assumes any responsibility or liability whatsoever on the behalf of the purchaser or reader of this material. Any perceived slight of any individual or organization is purely unintentional.

DEDICATION

*For all the wonderful patients and health care providers
who helped fight the traditional health care system
so they could take charge of their lives
and positively impact so many more.*

FOREWORD

by Janet Needham, R.Ph.

Early in my senior year of high school, I knew I wanted to become a pharmacist.

I wanted to help make a difference in people's health.

In the beginning of my journey as a provider, I embraced the norm. It was not until my husband, Shawn, also a pharmacist, realized we were part of the problem of the health care crisis that we embraced the "Wellness Model". Sick care is where our country is right now.

Before I graduated from pharmacy school in 1992, Heart Disease was the number one cause of death in the United States. Decades later, it still trumps any other cause. Our American lifestyle is not a healthy one – in fact, it has become deadly.

Our family was on the same path. The wake-up call came when Shawn started to have high blood pressure and high cholesterol.

He decided to address the root cause of his issues. He lost weight and started to work out again, and his health returned without medications. The entire family followed his lead to live a healthy lifestyle. Our mission at our pharmacy changed, as well. If you are a health care provider, you need to set a good example first.

We believe the only way to turn the existing trend around in our country is to embrace personal responsibility.

Throwing more medication at chronic illness has not been successful.

As health care providers, we need to be honest with consumers and give them the tools they need. Proper DIET, EXERCISE, and REST are requirements to be healthy.

Shawn and I believe that the current model of health insurance is broken. The health care industry is focused on what an insurance company will pay them, and the consumer's needs are sadly lost. The consumer is the passenger, not the driver.

In my family, colon cancer screening is a priority.
My siblings and I started at 40.

The current recommendation is to start screening at the age of 50.

I am alive today because I addressed this issue.

The point being, we all have risks that need to be screened and addressed, and we may not fit into the current "recommended" standard. In order to be screened, I had to convince a doctor to perform the procedure.

Recently, my hairdresser told me she just saw a new doctor. She was allowed to ask THREE questions concerning her health at this appointment after all the intake boxes were checked off. This is a not a quality interaction. In order for the doctor to be paid, this was the current process.

This cannot be a positive for the health care provider or the consumer. What if she had more concerns? Well, she was told to schedule another appointment. Sadly, this is the new norm. It does not have to be, though.

Shawn and I have a passion for what we do.

On a professional level, it has been rewarding to educate and empower consumers to live healthy lives. We own a cash-only pharmacy, with no health insurance interference. This allows us to offer consumers lower prices and better service.

This journey is why this book was written.

CHAPTER 1 - THE DAY THAT CHANGED EVERYTHING

For as long as I live, my wife, Janet and I will never forget that day. A pivotal moment in our career that forever changed everything for us.

Back in 2001, a morbidly obese patient came into our pharmacy. She was on around 20 different medications, ranging from high blood pressure to diabetes to high cholesterol. And they were costing her...

Nothing.
We were creating no value in her life.
She didn't care who we were.
She didn't care about the medications.
She didn't care about how they worked, or anything related because it was costing her nothing.
That day, we realized that we were not doing her or her health any favors by giving her 20 different medications under these circumstances. What she most needed to do was to change her diet and lifestyle.

Now, in our health care industry, there are government programs. She had Medicaid, so yes, we got paid. Paid by You, the taxpayers. YOU paid thousands of dollars a month for this lady's medications, which was the system's solution to "help her."

20 Medications!

Now, if she had to pay thousands of dollars a month herself, would she have changed her habits?

Ate better?
Exercised?
Lost weight?
And as a result, would most of those diseases have gone away?

Yes, we believe she (and they) would have.

Here's a small, but huge example of how the free market works…

If the consumer is responsible to pay out of pocket, this empowers them to ask different questions and own their choices.

When consumers have choices (about everything), then it increases natural competition of the vendors. Competition decreases skyrocketing costs and increases quality of service.

For any medication this patient DID decide was, even in the short term, in her best interest, the $2000 bill would have significantly decreased. The bottom line is this – the free market would be better for her health.

Better health for herself, creating a positive ripple for her family and community.

Better quality because of competition.

Better for YOU, the taxpayer.

What really struck us like a 2x4 that day was this:

1. She wouldn't need the drugs if she'd change her diet and lifestyle.
2. WE were a part of the problem.
3. Janet and I decided to change our commitment, and thus, our system.

In 2002, my wife and I converted our pharmacy to 100% direct pay (no insurance billing), with a 100% commitment to enable others to actually better their health,

   ...which leads to better families,
   ...which leads to better communities.

Our eyes and hearts were forever opened. Our commitment is to be part of a positive solution. Period.

WE HAVE A RESPONSIBILITY

We believe that if we want patients to look at us as educators in their health, we have a responsibility to take our own seriously and set good examples. When patients are paying for services, they deserve to go to someone they can believe in. In much of our current system, patients do not go to a health care provider because they value and trust their opinion, but because they're a preferred provider chosen (not by the patient, but) by their insurance (or government) plan. This inherently promotes no incentive to the health care provider to improve the relationship with the patient or be a healthy example themselves.

How many stories have we each experienced where the provider wasn't very personable or obviously not in great health? Would health care providers treat patients better if their patients were paying the bill? Would they be better examples of health?

Don't take this the wrong way. If I have a heart attack or am in a car wreck, by all means do what you can to save me. But as far as chronic disease management, I do not trust the system. It promotes sick patients and not healthy ones.

Ask yourself this: Would you go to a dentist with yellow crooked teeth if you were paying out of pocket to have some work done?

I rest my case…

I understand first-hand the real struggles that come with less than optimal health.

Know that you're not alone and that there's great news for affordable choices for those empowered to improve.

MY STORY

I struggled with my weight after my power lifting days, experiencing high blood pressure and high cholesterol. The doctors wanted to treat me with medications, but I decided that there must be a better way. After diet modifications, I lost 60 pounds, and both my high blood pressure and high cholesterol were gone!

Proper nutrition and hormone balancing gave my body the necessary tools to achieve optimal health and wellness.

WHY PHARMACY AND WHY COMPOUNDING?

When I was a high school sophomore, my Advanced Chemistry teacher recommended the direction of Pharmacy for me. I loved the idea of being employed in a small town with the opportunity to own my own business. Because of my passion for chemistry and helping people, it was a natural yes.

My wife, Janet, grew up on a farm in North Dakota as one of six children. She learned early the value of hard work and what it meant to care for others, which developed into a passion to help others in the area of health and wellness.

So, what IS compounding? It's the ability to customize the strength and dosage of drugs for the best possible outcome for the patient. We love this kind of pharmaceutical work since it allows us to work directly with our patients to contribute in a positive way towards their best health.

We're not tied to specific medications that are popular or pushed by the pharmaceutical companies but rather have complete control to customize the exact needs of our patients. It's a fulfilling win–win as we both have a direct stake in their short-and long-term health.

Janet and I are committed to changing lives through compounding and wellness, solving problems pharmaceutical companies can't, changing the way others view pharmacists, and being educators and promoters of health and wellness.

We are not insurance billers, nor promoters or enablers of poor health choices.

Janet and I believe in making families stronger and making a difference in people's lives. It's what we do.

THE PULL

As the years went by, I continued to notice things in my industry – with my patients and first-hand experiences as well as with stories of others – that I've come to know as the problem today. It's quite disturbing and alarming, and I just couldn't ignore the pull to educate any longer.

In this book, I will go through the history of our health care system and how we ended up here. The even better part is there is a solution and YOU are part of it.

CHAPTER 2 - THE PROBLEM TODAY

Whenever one segment of an economy exhibits, year after year, inflation above the general rate, and when there is no constraint on supply, then either a cartel is in operation or there is a lack of price transparency — or both, as is the case with American medical care."[1]

— JOHN STEELE GORDON

Everywhere we look, it seems, we find news, hear of scary trends, experience and hear stories of what's happening with our health care today.

So, what's true and what's not? I was compelled to do my own research, and here's what I found. Narrowing it down, we'll take a look at two overall things: health care trends and choices.

Here we go...

HEALTH CARE TRENDS

When it comes to health care trends, there were four very glaring areas that jumped out! Specifically:

1. Costs
2. Quality
3. Overutilization, and
4. The Most Alarming Trend

My intention with these is to highlight each one to make the point versus go too much in depth and risk losing you (and me)!

COSTS

Most of the following stats come as no surprise as I interact with my patients on a daily basis.

According to Wikipedia, "a major trend in employer sponsored coverage has been increasing premiums, deductibles, and co~payments for medical services."[2]

According to Becker's Hospital CFO Report:

- 67% of families are very worried or somewhat worried about the ability to afford unexpected medical bills for them or their family.
- 1 in 3 GoFundMe campaigns are medical fundraisers.
- 57% received a bill they thought would be covered by insurance (most common were physician services and lab tests).
- 53% are worried about affording their health insurance deductible.

- Over 40% are worried about affording prescription drugs.[3]

Are you nodding your head already?! Yup, you're not alone!

According to health system tracker, "1 in 4 people taking prescription drugs report difficulty affording their medication."[4]

And this headline should come as no surprise for those that have or know someone with this deadly disease...

Cancer Survivors Face Significant Hardships Related to Medical Bills

Jan. 21, 2019 — New research indicates that cancer survivors carry greater financial burdens related to medical debt payments and bills compared with individuals without a cancer history, with the greatest hardships ... **read more** »

And it's no surprise why – check this out:
Everywhere we look in the news, including online, outrageous sounding medication costs are discussed. It's certainly a hot topic! According to a news article on Katu.com about Vitraki, a "breakthrough" cancer-specific drug that comes at a very "steep price":

The cost for the children's syrup is $11,000/month.
Oral capsules for adults are $32,000/month.[5]

The Washington Post reports,
Specialty drugs lead the way with eye-popping price tags — current therapies for hemophilia are priced at $580,000 to $800,000 a year; Novartis plans a $475,000 price tag for its Car-T drug Kymriah, which treats non-Hodgkin's lymphoma.[6]

What?! Yes, these are simply crazy!

The below stats seem to be "normal" and "common practice" with our current system. Are you included in this?

Many Americans have received an unexpected medical bill. A survey of more than 1,000 people conducted at the University of Chicago found 57 percent of respondents had received a medical bill they thought would be covered by insurance. The most common services they were charged for were physician services and laboratory tests.[7]

According to PwC, prices continue to be the primary driver of health care spending, growing at a faster rate than utilization.[8]

Wow!

Costs are rising and the average American today is *very concerned* about the affordability of health care for themselves and their family. And how is this possible if we're supposedly the richest nation in the world?!

QUALITY

There are really two specific challenges when it comes to the quality of the health care we're receiving in our current system. In my research, I (not surprisingly) discovered:

1. According to Consumer Reports, "the typical primary physician today devotes just 15 minutes to patient visits,"[9] and
2. According to a Medscape report, "among physician respondents, 42% reported burnout and 15% admitted to depression.[10]

https://www.medscape.com/slideshow/2018-lifestyle-burnout-depression-6009235

Eye opening, right?! Many of us have experienced the effects and won't be surprised by these statistics. What does this mean for us? If physicians are burned out, depressed, and not spending much time with us, how is it remotely possible that the quality of care we receive is high?

You're right… it's not. This is a serious trend with our current health care system.

This IS today's reality. The good news is, it doesn't have to be our future.

OVERUTILIZATION

Before I dive into more on this trend, I'd like to first share a portion of a fascinating educational (and entertaining) analogy about why health care costs keep rising with this YouTube video featuring Dinesh D'Souza found in Resources:

Why do health care costs keep rising? For a really simple reason.

The guy who's getting the benefit is not the guy who's paying.

Now, let me engage in a moment of speculative, progressive reasoning for a moment.

We have a right (no less for health care) to eat.
We have a right to food. Who would deny that the right to prevent ourselves from starvation is as basic a right as health care?

Alright, now let's apply (the government's running of health care) as it applies to food.

You will now be allowed to go to the grocery store and order whatever you want.
Fill up your cart.
You don't have to pay.
Somebody else will pay.
What's going to happen?
The first thing that will happen is that you'll take all kinds of stuff you don't need.
You'll fill your cart. You'll buy 12 cartons of milk and 45 cartons of bologna.
And then you'll go up to the counter and
the grocery store will realize that they can charge whatever they want.

Because you're not paying.
So they will escalate their prices.

So what's going on with free health care is that the taxpayer is being ripped off to give so called "free stuff."

Does this sound absurd to you? A bit cheeky perhaps? Yup, it does to me as well. However, the principles in this analogy have been nailed down.

In my research, we ran across a study published on the National Center for Biotechnology Information's public website[11] (U.S. National Library of Medicine). According to the study's findings, a whopping 20.6% of overall medical care was unnecessary. Including:

- 22% of prescription medications
- 24.9% of tests
- 11.1% of procedures[12]

What?! Very surreal.

The most common cited reasons for overtreatment were:

- 84.7% fear of malpractice
- 59.0% patient pressure/request

These were quoted directly from the findings! And represent the top two answers. These are the hard stats, folks! The raw and simple truth.

Let's break it down a bit more. Who does the fear of malpractice come from?

Yup, you're right – the patients.

Again, if the patient were paying directly versus having someone else pay the bill, would this still happen? My gut says no. If the patient was paying, it's not difficult to make the argument that the number of malpractice suits would drop significantly. Why? Because the doctor would have more time to spend creating a relationship with the patient. When the patient feels understood, and the decisions are joint, then it stands to reason that there will be less cause for anger over the result.

Regarding unnecessary medical care, this triggered my memory with a story from our early days in pharmacy:

Back then, we were working with and billing DME (Durable Medical Equipment) as fulfillment to set up oxygen for patients.

We always did 90-day follow-ups on patients, because Medicare required that we do this to ensure they were compliant.

During a particular follow-up, we realized that the patient had not used the oxygen at all.

We were billing Medicare $300 per month for the oxygen that hadn't been used.

So, per the rules, we were directed by Medicare to pick it up, since they're not using it, and take it back.

We tried to do just that, and the patient said,

"Well, I'm not using it, but I want it there just in case I need it."

I was accustomed to working in the hospital, and if someone was on oxygen, it was because they were in dire need.

And if they didn't have it, they would die.

So, here this patient is not using the oxygen. We're charging Medicare $300 per month.

It's costing the patient nothing.

And they want to keep it.

Why?

Because it was costing them nothing and the taxpayer was paying the bill.

Can you see why Janet and I decided to change our business model?! Just because we weren't involved in the decision-making process regarding the patient's *actual need*, we still were a part of this crazy system, and not contributing towards their best health.

Overutilization is precisely what is happening daily and every-where in the US with our current healthcare system.

Overutilization by patients.
- They're not paying for it, so why would they care?

Overutilization by healthcare providers.
- The patient isn't paying the bill, so what's the harm?
OR
- I don't want to get sued, so I'll just give them what they want. Again, in the end, they're not paying for it anyway, so what's the harm?

Because the taxpayer or insurance company is footing the bill and not the end user, overutilization is occurring by consumers, and some health care providers are able to get away with shady-feeling, non-transparent pricing that they'd never get away with in the "real business world" so to speak.

When consumers are paying, they're put in the driver's seat for making decisions. They'll factor in price, quality, location, customer service, and whatever other factors are important to them personally.

Competition for business happens daily when it comes to our discretionary spending, whether it's at which store to buy clothes or where to get a haircut, purchase a flat screen TV or furniture, vacations, restaurants, massages, etc. Why should the care of our health be any different?

I don't believe it should and it doesn't have to.

THE MOST ALARMING TREND

For the majority of Americans, this eye-opening trend will come as no surprise, but it almost seems like the elephant in the room. Treating the symptoms and not the root cause will never truly lead to a person with optimal health. Never. It gives people a false sense of hope and can have devastating mental consequences that have a ripple effect throughout their lives when not properly addressed.

So, what am I talking about?

Obesity.

First, to set the stage, "U.S. health care spending increased 3.9 percent to reach $3.5 trillion, or $10,739 per person in 2017."[13]

And check this out:

> According to "a new Milken Institute report, U.S. health care costs for chronic diseases such as heart disease, cancer, diabetes, and Alzheimer's disease totaled $1.1 trillion in 2016. When lost economic productivity is included, the total economic impact was $3.7 trillion. This is equivalent to nearly ***20 percent*** of the U.S. gross domestic product.[14]

> In terms of risk factors, being overweight or obese accounted for $1.7 trillion, or ***47 percent*** of the total cost. Approximately 8.7 percent of health-care spending in the U.S. is attributable to cigarette smoking; 60 percent of that is paid by public sources — Medicare, Medicaid, and other U.S. federal and state health programs.[15] Health problems caused by excessive drinking cost $27.4 billion in 2010, or 1 percent of the total cost of chronic diseases and 11 percent of the total cost of alcohol abuse.

> American adults classified as obese increased from 13 percent in 1960 to almost 40 percent in 2016. Another 33 percent are overweight. Epidemiologic research has established a strong link between obesity and chronic diseases such as heart disease, kidney disease, and several types of cancers."[16]

Whoa! Talk about a very serious and alarming trend today!

The good news is that there IS hope for a better, healthier future. However, awareness is the first step.

Which leads me to…

CHOICES

The current system most Americans are utilizing right now for the primary care of their health has been in place and accepted as commonplace for either all or most of their lives.

Here's how it works...

1. You purchase insurance through either your employer (yes, even if the employer provides it, you are paying for it), former employer, or a 3rd party or directly from the government.
2. They have specific approved doctors, specialists, clinics, and hospitals.
3. You use only from the approved list or they're not covered (regardless of quality, price, whether you connect with them, etc.).
4. You pay a co-pay.
5. You may or may not receive a random, unexpected bill after the fact, despite having no up-front transparency of the potential charges.
6. You either spend tons of time and energy going back and forth trying to clarify; OR
7. You just pay it, feel yucky, and be done.

Sound familiar?

Here's the problem today: Most consumers think they have no choice.

They think that they have to settle for whatever the doctor, insurance company, or government has previously approved and follow the above very likely scenario.

The other problem today is that consumers don't think or don't know that there IS another, better way.

I've gotten so frustrated over the years seeing the insanity of the same loop with the same results with not only my pharmacy patients, but with my family, friends, and acquaintances, too, that I decided to do some research (20+ years to be precise). I decided that enough is enough. There HAS to be a better way.

And do you know what?

An affordable alternative DOES exist, and not only does it exist, but parts are based on a system that's been in place for decades, meaning it has already proven to work!

Before we dive into what could happen if we DON'T make different choices, it's important to take an overview look at what specifically has happened in the past that has led us to this exact moment in time.

Today is an immensely critical time in our nation, where not only is the government's involvement creating a devastating environment for future generations, but ALSO a time of awakening and empowerment of the American people to take back control, to put our natural entrepreneurial armor on and create more solutions for sustainable health, happiness, families, and communities.

This is not a pipe dream and really can be done! There IS hope for a better future.

The problem is this… without looking back at history first, we'll never truly learn from the past and create a real, sustainable future for our families and communities.

So here we go… let's Look Back to Move Forward.

27

CHAPTER 3 - LOOKING BACK TO MOVE FORWARD

> *"Those who do not learn history are doomed to repeat it."*

> — GEORGE SANTAYANA

The best way to really understand the premise behind my claim that the Government has ruined health care is to look back at four specific points in history. I could write a book on each of these and more, but for the purposes of this book, we'll look at the following four in a bit more detail.

Also, a brief disclaimer: For those of you who's eyes glaze over when reading about facts, I can empathize. For us both, I've kept it as brief, organized, and relevant as I can – just long enough to make my point and to showcase that this is not a one-time challenge, but a long, huge track record in history. There are many more examples, but I've chosen these four that I believe act as milestones.

Here are the four milestones that we'll take a closer look at:

1. The Social Security Act, signed by President Roosevelt on August 14th, 1935
2. Executive Order 9328, signed by President Roosevelt on April 8th, 1943
3. The Social Security Amendments of 1965, signed by President Johnson on July 30th, 1965, and
4. The Patient Protection and Affordable Care Act (ACA), signed by President Obama on March 23rd, 2010

THE SOCIAL SECURITY ACT OF 1935

The purpose of this act, signed by President Roosevelt on August 14th, 1935 was to provide a basic pension to those in old age and to provide insurance to those who were unemployed. The Social Security Act was one of eleven acts or programs of Roosevelt's Second New Deal.[1]

So, what was the significance of this decision in history?

This particular act was a major milestone in history because it fundamentally changed the relationship between the federal government and the individual citizens. It truly planted the seed in our minds of how society and government should function together, including paving the way and setting a precedence for government interference regarding choices for the individual citizen.

EXECUTIVE ORDER 9328 OF 1943

Executive Order 9328 was a result of the Stabilization Act of 1942, enacted October 2nd, 1942, to attempt to help control inflation and other prices. This did include the stabilization of wages and salaries to levels as of September 15th, 1942,[2] but it wasn't until President Roosevelt issued Executive Order 9328 on April 8th,

1943, that he mandated the indefinite freeze on wages and salaries.[3]

Interestingly, back in 1935, the Supreme Court said that minimum wage laws were unconstitutional. Why? They interfered with an employer's ability to freely negotiate wage contracts with employees.

Yes. Government interference is really the key phrase here.

So here we are now, with executive powers enabling wage and salary freezes nationwide. This was definitely not what the founding fathers intended when they wrote the Constitution. The intent was to empower the American people by putting free market principles to work and to keep government to a bare minimum. If it was meant to be the duty of the federal government, it would have been expressly included in the Constitution.

> *"The powers not delegated to the United States by the Constitution, nor prohibited by it to the States, are reserved to the States respectively, or to the people."*

So, what happened as a result?

1. Employer-sponsored health insurance plans expanded and were offered as a direct result of the wage controls imposed by the federal government, and
2. The snowball effect gains momentum

Employer-Sponsored Health Insurance
Since the federal government was tying the hands of employers nationwide, the only way to attract and retain the best employees was to think outside the box. Because they couldn't touch wages or salaries, the option of offering benefits really took off in the

coming years. The case that this may not have happened if employers could have made their own decision to raise wages is very easy to make. It's a simple case of the market responding to a need.

In fact, by 1951, employers started to become the dominant third-party insurance buyer.

Why should we care?

This is a huge milestone, setting a precedent for a third party stepping in between the consumer and the care of their health. It helped to establish the "new normal" and the beginning of the mentality that perhaps someone else should pay.

The Snowball Effect Gains Momentum
Since the door had been cracked for government control, it wasn't a surprise that in both 1945 and 1949, President Truman was actively promoting the idea of nationalizing health care.

The American Medical Association (AMA), as a result, conducted the most expensive[4] lobbying effort to date, opposing Truman's nationalized health care ideas. So, why did they oppose national health care? They called it "un-American" and "socialized medicine." (As an interesting side note, the Chamber of Commerce also referred to Truman's national health care system as socialism after his 1945 address!)

> *"The problem with socialism is that you eventually run out of other people's money."*
>
> — MARGARET THATCHER

In 1961, Ronald Reagan spoke out against socialized medicine. He *"criticized Social Security for supplanting private savings and warned that subsidized medicine would curtail Americans' freedom"* and that *"pretty soon your son won't decide when he's in school, where he will go or what he will do for a living. He will wait for the government to tell him."*[5]

The later claim may have sounded a bit dramatic at the time, but the principle is sound. The frustration was that the government was going to control and interfere with direct consumer choices. Our freedom was being threatened, and the Chamber of Commerce, Ronald Reagan, and the American Medical Association (among others) were willing to stand up for our freedom of choice, a fundamental right.

After all, it had already started. They wanted to take a stand and attempt to stop the leak before it became a flood.

On May 20th, 1962, Edward Annis, the president of the AMA, delivered a televised response to President Kennedy's address saying that Medicare would *"put the government smack into your hospital."*

Why should we care?

The reality is that the government would have control over what doctors, hospitals, medicines, procedures, and patients can and can't do versus the doctor and patient discussing, collaborating, and deciding on the next steps based on what's best for the patient versus the rules and regulations as dictated by the government.

It all comes down to...

Control.

Choices.

Freedom.

THE SOCIAL SECURITY AMENDMENTS OF 1965

The Social Security Amendments of 1965 were signed by President Johnson on July 30th, 1965.[6] Their purpose was to provide health insurance to the elderly (Medicare, a federal program) and for the poor (Medicaid, a state program with matching dollars from the federal government based on income). Medicare and Medicaid were the two largest programs that were created as a direct result of these amendments. They were the first public health insurance programs in the U.S. and were a ***monumental milestone*** and precedent for beginning an era focused on health programs controlled by the government.

What was previously seen as un-American and socialism is now the new reality with dire consequences to come. This new era of government control in health care, although enacted with the best of intentions, is now in motion to set a precedent of acceptance as the new normal.

So, what happened as a result?

1. The U.S. Health Care Cost Crisis started in 1965, and
2. The Snowball Effect Gains Momentum.

The U.S. Health Care Cost Crisis Started in 1965
Do you remember back to Chapter 2 when I referred to the story about Free Food and how the costs would artificially rise when the payer isn't the one benefitting? This is precisely what happened.

The US government created a buyer monopoly as a direct result after creating Medicare and Medicaid both. Since the end user was not paying for the care, why not be seen for as many things as you'd like? This artificially increased demand due to overutilization. (Buy whatever you like, right?!)

See the Figure 1 chart below.[7] Health care prices responded at twice the rate of inflation

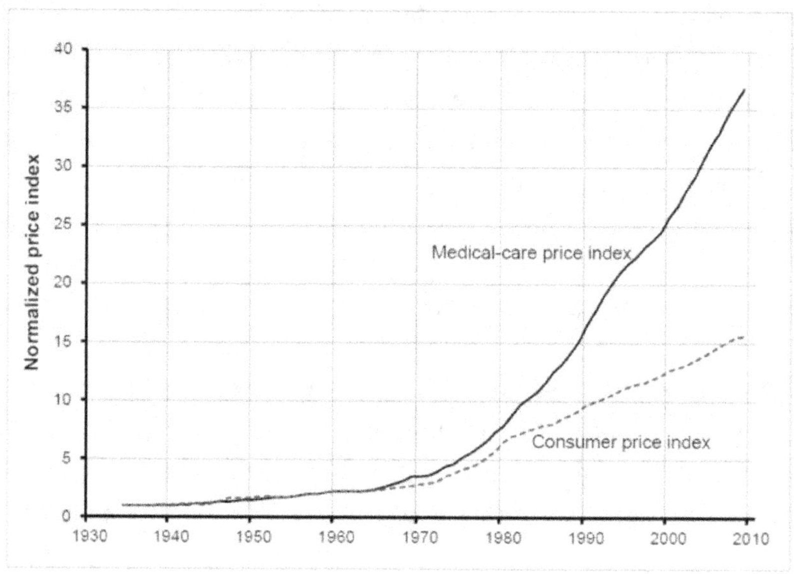

Figure 1

Why should we care?

It comes down to sustainability. How long could this possibly be sustainable? Without a free market that includes competition in place to keep prices in check, why would inflation suddenly slow? This is extremely dangerous. Also, without free market principles (a.k.a. entrepreneurial, innovative, competitive businesses) working for our collective benefit, our choices are incredibly limited. As consumers, we've grown so accustomed to this being the "normal" that we've forgotten that We Have Choices.

The Snowball Effect Gains Momentum

According to the Mises Institute, "by the 1980s the U.S. was restricting the supply of physicians, hospitals, insurance, pharmaceuticals, while subsidizing demand. Since then, the US has been trying to control high costs by moving toward something perhaps best described by the House Budget Committee:

> *In too many areas of the economy – especially energy, finance, and health care – free enterprise has given way to government control in "partnership" with a few large or politically well-connected companies (Ryan 2012)."*

After the government created Medicare and Medicaid, the next step was to create the rules and regulations by which everyone is required to play (should they choose to become a part of the system. Yes. Everyone Has Choices.). Those rules and regulations included (yes, you guessed it) doctors, hospitals, insurance, surgeries, procedures, pharmaceuticals, etc.

In 1984, prescription drug monopolies strengthened after the Drug Price Competition and Patent Term Restoration Act permitted the extension of patents beyond 20 years.

Courtesy of Statista.com check out this graphic on Prescription drug expenditures in the United States from 1960 to 2018 (in billion U.S. dollars).[8] Talk about alarming!

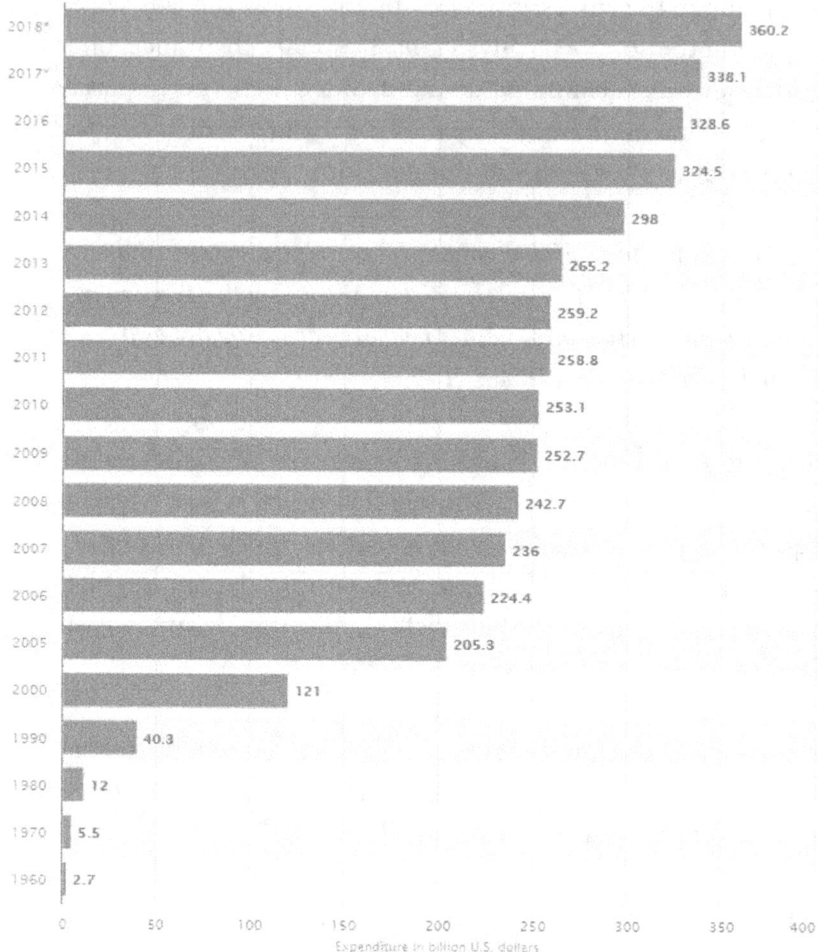

Yowza, right?! The astronomical increases are sick, certainly not part of a free market system, and completely not sustainable.

In 2003, prescription drug monopolies were yet again strengthened after the Medicare Prescription Drug, Improvement, and Modernization Act provided subsidies. Medicare Part D, covering a portion of prescription drugs, took effect Jan 1st, 2006. We can see below what happened as a result.

Courtesy of data from the AARP Public Policy Institute, check out the Average Annual Prescription Drug Inflation versus the Annual CPI-U:[9]

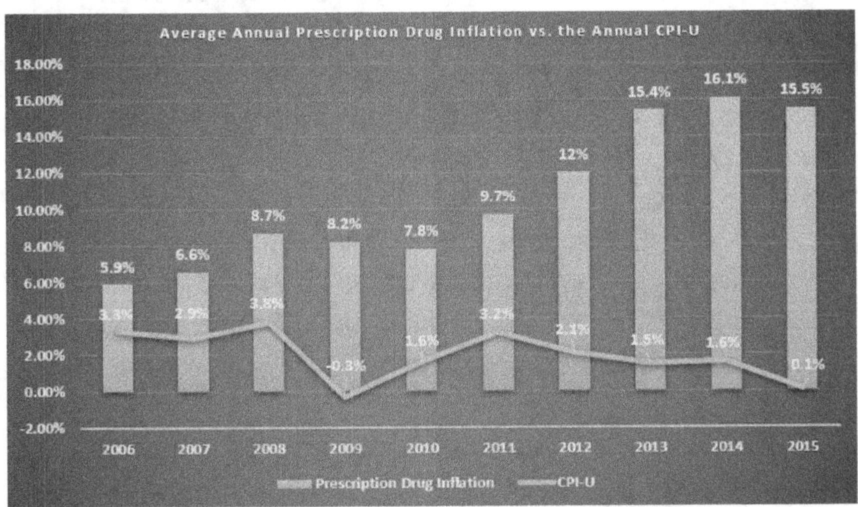

As is clearly apparent here, the overall trend of prescription drug inflation is an incredible upward, very high trend. When we compare this trend to the Consumer Price Index, it's extremely alarming.

Why is this a problem for us all?

When the government "pays" for medication (a.k.a., YOU, the taxpayer), drug companies and pharmacies no longer have to work for competitive pricing. Again, the end user isn't footing the bill, so the pricing becomes inflated. This is most definitely NOT a win–win scenario, at least not for us consumers. In the short term, it may sound good for those on the federal programs. However, the reality is that it makes it more expensive for everyone and someone has to pay for it in higher taxes (the government doesn't generate revenue from anywhere else but through taxes).

THE PATIENT PROTECTION AND AFFORDABLE CARE ACT (ACA) OF 2010 (A.K.A. "OBAMACARE")

During research on this Act signed by President Obama on March 23rd, 2010, it's generally agreed and accepted that this act represents the single most influential overall of the health insurance system controlled by the federal government since the Amendments of 1965.

What's also interesting is that the act appears to be so complex that even in the Wikipedia version, the express purpose is not clear. As a result of plenty of research, I believe this to be the most clear and succinct explanation of the purpose behind it.

1. Provide health "insurance" to more people
2. Expand the Medicaid program
3. Overhaul delivery methods to cut costs (a.k.a.: rationing)

So, what was the significance of this decision in history?

One of the provisions included in the act mandated everyone to participate or pay a tax penalty. Wow, talk about coming a long way since the early days of 100% consumer choices! Unfortunately, the early opposers' fear of nationalized health care was not only realized but it exploded in a **big way** with the enactment of the ACA. Government control is at its all-time high as a result.

So, what did happen as a result? Let's take a look at...

1. Overall Health Care Expenditures. Did they go down?
2. Average Monthly Premiums
and ask the question...
3. Has a Judge Ruled it Unconstitutional?

Overall Health Care Expenditures

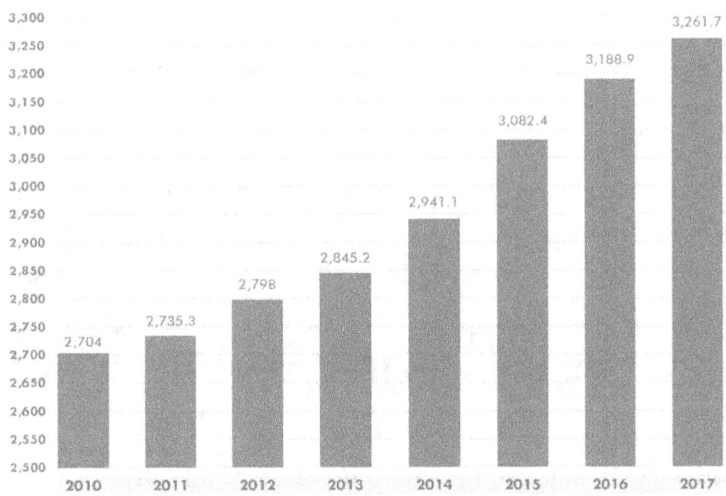

Sickened: How the Government Ruined Healthcare and How to Fix It.
Facebook.com/SickenedTheBook

From 2009 to 2014, the National Health Expenditures as a percent of GDP held steady at 17.3% (with one exception in 2013, where it was a mere 17.2%. Interestingly, in 1980, it was 8.9%, almost half!). In 1990, it was 12.1% and in 2000 it was 13.4%. In 2015, 2016, and 2017, it was 17.6%, 18%, & 17.9% respectively.[10] As you can clearly see from this graphic, no, health expenditures did NOT go down as a result of passing the ACA in 2010 and implementing the majority of the plan in 2014. In fact, there's a significant uptrend!

Average Monthly Premiums
According to eHealthInsurance, health insurance premiums have risen since the inception of the ACA.

Here are the average monthly premiums for individuals.

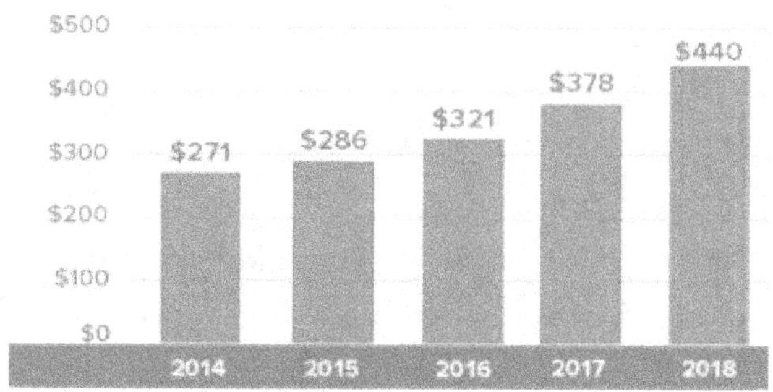

From 2014 to 2018, there's been an increase of just over 62%. This is with an average deductible of $4,578.

So, what about families? Here are the average monthly premiums for family coverage.

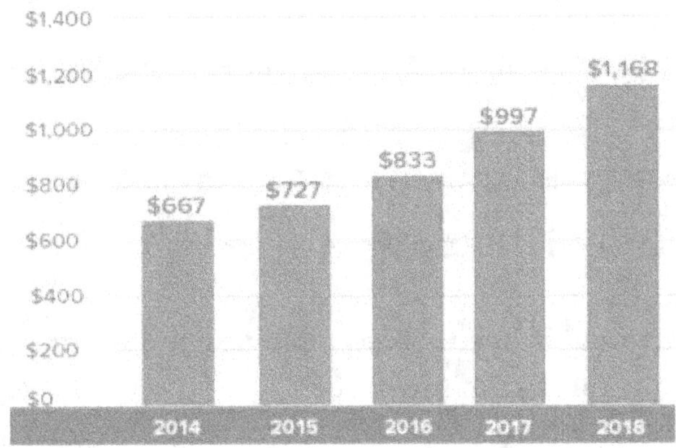

From 2014 to 2018, this is an increase in just over 75% for families! This is with an average family deductible of $8,803. Wow!

So, have overall expenditures been cut as a result of the ACA? Nope. As you can clearly see for yourself here, they've actually increased due to the lack of a free market system (competition) when it comes to health care. The more the government gets involved, the more expensive it gets.

Has a Judge Ruled the Act Unconstitutional?
As of January 2019, Yes.

According to CNBC, late Dec 14th, 2017, US District Court Judge Reed O'Connor declared that key portions of the ACA are "inconsistent with the US Constitution."[11] "O'Connor's ruling argued that the health-care law cannot stand on its own since Congress last December repealed the individual mandate, which imposed a tax penalty on consumers who went uninsured."

Yup, that's right. Now the government is telling us what to do regarding our health care.

Government Mandates = Revocation of (Choices + Freedom).

AN ABSURD EXAMPLE (OR IS IT?)

Humor me in considering for a moment...

What would happen if our employers bought auto insurance like they buy our health insurance?

Let me give you an example...

Ok, you wreck your car.

> *Oh wow, my car is destroyed!*
> *What am I going to do?*
> *But that's ok! It'll be alright.*
> *My employer bought car insurance for me.*

So, instead of having to pay because your car is wrecked, you go into the repair shop, and your employer's auto insurance pays for it.

Well.... The next thing you know... you need new tires.

So, you go to your local tire store.

And you say...

> *Wait a minute!*
> *$1000 for new tires?!*
> *This is ridiculous!*

My employer's auto insurance should cover this!

So… you get your employer's auto insurance to cover this, too.

The next thing you know… you're getting your brakes changed… and you quickly think…

Holy Smokes! This is going to be like, $400!
I should not have to pay out of pocket for this!
My employer's auto insurance should pay for this!

So… guess what… just like that, your employer's auto insurance covers your brakes.

And now, we're going to get even more absurd…

You're filling up your gas tank, and you think…

You know what? This is ridiculous!
I'm paying $50 out of MY Pocket!
My employer's auto insurance should cover my gas.

Well, guess what?

That is exactly where our health care system has gone.

It started out as major medical, hospital insurance.

Now we get everything covered from our routine doctor visits, to our dental visits, to our glasses, to our stubbed toes, to our ingrown toenails, to our children's diaper rash (you get the picture).

That's where our health care has gone.

And... why it's so expensive.

Because Someone Else Is Paying The Bill.

Most of the time, be it the government, insurance, or employers, they do.

So… What if they DID pay our auto insurance? What if this was our reality?

Would we specifically go out and try and wreck our cars so we could get things paid for?

No, we wouldn't.

Well… not that some people wouldn't give it some serious thought, though, right? (That's not a stretch.)

But, do you know what?

That's **exactly** what some people have done with their health.

They specifically do not take care of themselves because someone else is paying the bill. Some consciously and some, subconsciously, because of how the system is set up and has trained their thinking.

Imagine... if we *ALL* actually did that with our cars.

CONCLUSION

When I first began sharing with select people that I was writing this book, they immediately jumped to "ObamaCare." This is completely understandable since this is what they know and has been the focus of our most recent history regarding the health insurance discussion.

However, I've been very well aware for over 20 years that there is more to it than that. The U.S. government, throughout our history, has not only set dangerous precedents but an incredibly huge snowball effect of control and interference with our choices as consumers, and with our freedom as U.S. citizens. And we're the ones paying for it – with outrageous pricing, poor quality care, and way too often very poor customer experiences.

Yes, they have indeed ruined health care for us Americans. Their decisions have had numerous snowball effects and ramifications that have had a direct ripple effect across many segments of the American economy. We're so used to this new "normal" that most blindly accept as having no choice. Some feel a lack of empower-ment to be able to DO anything.

When our Founding Fathers wrote the Constitution, their inten-tion was yes, to help American citizens with the protection of life, liberty, and the pursuit of happiness. They knew that within the true American spirit lies the drive, work ethic, and passion to create a better life for ourselves, our families, and future generations.

In true entrepreneurial spirit, we Americans are incredibly innov-ative, creative, positive, and determined to see a true need in our society and then to work together for the purpose of filling it for the betterment of all.

When the government continually takes away our freedom of choice, the end result is a mess. History has clearly shown that. Instead of trusting in the true American spirit to innovate and take care of each other, the government instead (by this history trail) has effectively said:

> *I don't trust you. You're the child that can't think or do anything for yourself, so just let Big Daddy "take care" of you instead. Trust me. After all, I'm giving you "Affordable Health Care."*

Clearly nothing is even remotely close to being "affordable" when it comes to the government's way of doing things. Should we trust them with the future of our care? To solve these issues?

Are we doomed to continue working to "keep our insurance" just to maintain a so-called "quality of life"?

No, my friends, we are not.

There is hope for a better way.

But before I share that, we should carefully consider…

What happens if a solution isn't found?

CHAPTER 4 - WHAT HAPPENS IF WE DON'T MAKE DIFFERENT CHOICES?

> *"The only complicated things worth fighting for will change the world in some way."*

> — INGRID WEIR

My grandma was 80 years old at the time.

In great overall health and walking four miles a day on her treadmill. After about three miles on the treadmill, she got tired, so she made an appointment and talked to her primary care doctor.

Knowing that there's a new cardiac unit in town, her doctor referred her to the cardiologist.

She made an appointment, spoke with the cardiologist, and the cardiologist ("shockingly") said,

"Well, Mrs. Crawford, you have a heart murmur. You have a leaking valve and we need to replace it."

I recommended that she not have the surgery.

Her son (my uncle) recommended that she not have the surgery.

She did it anyway.

The doctor told her,

> *"Mrs. Crawford, Medicare will cover it. You don't have to worry about any kind of payment in this situation. Medicare will cover it."*

So, she went into the hospital and in the operating room, she codes… Meaning she almost dies.

They had to do CPR to revive her. For anybody, but especially for an 80-year-old woman, this is very, very stressful.

She ends up in the ICU for two weeks, then in a nursing home for a month.

She was very lucky she lived.

Medicare paid for all of this, which was hundreds of thousands of dollars.

My belief is that if we didn't have government insurance (and all health insurance is government insurance now, because of the regulations placed on them by the government) that paid for this, it would have never been done.

I believe it was an unnecessary procedure on a healthy 80-year-old old woman.

I believe that it was pushed by the cardiologist who unfortunately saw dollar signs for the new unit.

I was outraged.

I think, if we all live to be 80, we should be happy to walk four miles a day on the treadmill, even if we get tired after three miles! And I believe her doctor failed in his responsibility to tell her that.

Why did he fail? He deferred the decision and responsibility to the cardiologist.

I believe that if the free market had been involved, the doctor would have given her options, and she would have decided *for herself* if she wanted to go through with surgery or not. Mind you there would be a monetary expense involved and that would play into the decision as well (and that is a good thing).

And knowing my grandma, if she had to pay for the service, she probably would have just lived with "only" walking 3 miles on the treadmill per day. That decision would have saved a lot of resources and not put her health at risk, not to mention her recovery time.

~

WE ALL HAVE CHOICES.

Even when we feel we don't, we actually do. We have choices to say yes to the doctor's advice. We have choices to seek a second opinion. We have choices to ask further questions regarding our health or that of our family members – especially, to not let a health insurance company make these choices for us.

With the problems that we as Americans are facing today regarding health care as well as the very clear troubling government history, we absolutely have the choice to make changes, to seek other viable solutions…

… AND we retain the choice to stay the course and just do what we're told… just like my grandmother.

After all, change isn't always easy, right?

Let's imagine for a moment that we choose to stay the course, follow our current system, and continue to do what we're told. Or in other words, not take full responsibility for our health choices. (I know, no longer appealing, right?) Let's just stick with this idea for the moment and follow the paths of three other countries and see how government run health care has fared for them, shall we?

FIRST, LET'S TAKE A LOOK AT RUSSIA.

According to Wikipedia… "Due to the ongoing Russian financial crisis since 2014, major cuts in health spending have resulted in a decline in the quality of service of the state health care system. About 40% of basic medical facilities have fewer staff than they are supposed to have, with others being closed down. Waiting periods for treatment have increased, and patients have been forced to pay for more services that were previously free."[1]

HOW ABOUT OUR FRIENDLY CANADIAN NEIGHBORS?

According to a 2018 report by The Fraser Institute "Waiting for treatment has become a defining characteristic of Canadian health care."[2] Here are some fascinating statistics regarding their average wait times…

- 8.7 weeks between a referral and specialist consultation
- 10.6 weeks for an MRI
- 11 weeks between a consultation with a specialist and when treatment starts
- 19.8 weeks between a referral and receipt of medically necessary treatment
- 39 weeks between a referral and orthopedic surgery

UP LAST, LET'S TAKE A LOOK AT CUBA'S HEALTH CARE...

In our research, we found nightmare stories...

- Requiring patients to bring their own bed sheets and light bulbs[3]
- Facilities not being updated or without basic hygiene[4]
- Women with high-risk pregnancies often encouraged, or forced, to get an abortion[5]
- Lacking personnel to collect dirty dishes or keep the floor, which orthopedic patients walk along, dry[6]
- Chronic shortages of medicines and low wages lead to the black market[7]
- A two-tier system, one for the foreign guest and Cuban insiders (like Castro and his "cronies," according to the Washington Examiner)[8]and one for everybody else

Did you also know that when Fidel Castro was sick, his government paid to fly in a Spanish specialist along with medical equipment not available in Cuba?[9] That decision doesn't put much optimism in the Cuban health care system. It's a prime example of what not to do!

Wow, these don't paint a great picture. As awful as these sound, it's easy to think and say,

"That will never happen in OUR country!" (Right?!)

After all, we're smart, innovative, and supposedly the richest and most powerful country in the world, right? We would never let that happen to us.

Hmmm…

…So, what about us?

In 2018, the trustees of the Social Security Trust Fund reported that the program will become financially insolvent in the year 2034. Increased taxes or reduced coverage will be required. Supplementary Medical Insurance trust funds are also being seriously depleted and increased tax rates or reduced coverage will be required. [10]

The bottom line is that depending on the government for the care of our health is NOT sustainable, smart, good for us, or good for the future. Our system is already directly on track to succumb to all of the above outcomes that Russia, Canada, and Cuba have already devastatingly experienced.

This is our wake-up call.

This is our call to action.

It's time to take a stand and make a choice.

A choice to take full responsibility for our own health and for the health of our families and communities throughout our incredible nation.

It's perfectly fine if you don't have the entire picture yet. We all have choices. Join me and make the choice and stand right now for a better, more sustainable future.

In fact, I'd like for you to play along a bit longer with me. I'd like to take you to take a sneak peek into the future. I'd like for you to Imagine a World Where…

Let's Go.

CHAPTER 5 - IMAGINE A WORLD WHERE

The more that I've become aware of what's wrong in our lives when our health isn't right, the more I dream what it would actually be like to live in a world where we innately strive for our best health, to have the best energy, to do the activities we love or would love to try, to have the positive mental health and outlook to do more for our families and communities.

Imagine what would happen if positive health were the norm?

Imagine if our health care system actually focused on optimal health instead of sick care?

Let's imagine a world where...

You call your doctor directly because you have a sore throat. It's been hanging on for longer than comfortable and it's time to get it checked out.

OR

You send a text because, who are we kidding, we're just dropping off Justin for soccer practice before picking up Ashley from piano lessons!

Perfect! The doctor is happy to see you in about an hour, which will give you the ideal window to continue your day.

When you walk into the clinic, the doctor herself meets you at the door. The first few minutes are focused on catching up since you last visited. The atmosphere is calm, not rushed, and is focused on connecting with you, as fitting, before taking a look at your throat. She actually cares about YOU!

All in all, you're in and out in about 25 minutes with a prescription to solve the issue so you can move on with your day. On your way out, you happily pay the flat rate for the visit, $75, by swiping your card in the tablet, adding your signature, and you're off to your pharmacy.

Because you've done your prior research, you've decided your favorite pharmacy is a bit further away, but along with exceptional value you just love the personal touch they provide.

When you arrive at your pharmacy, you're greeted by first name, asked how Justin's enjoying his soccer season and how Ashley's first recital went (remembering the story last time about how nervous and excited she was!).

After handing over the new prescription, filling it on the spot for $15 via your debit card, you share that you've recently lost 30 pounds by clean eating and exercise. Feeling the positive momentum, you decided to start running but are now experiencing knee pain.

The health-conscious pharmacist explains that running is very high impact and is a common cause of knee problems, especially after the age of 50. He suggested lower impact biking, which is sustainable until well over 100!

He also recommends collagen protein to help build your knee up, in addition to a strength and core building, balance, and mobility routine.

You're feeling heard, taken care of, and hopeful once again as a result of both conversations from your neighborhood doctor and pharmacist! Your health care team is awesome!

So, what did you notice here? What was different?

First, yes, you read that correctly, YOU have the doctor's direct number and s/he is the one who greets you directly. Can you seriously imagine texting your doctor for an appointment?!

Why would the doctor greet you personally?

1. <u>Less Overhead For The Doctor.</u> Less staff is needed, since dealing with insurance is no longer a heavy anchor, as this is a cash-only clinic. She's streamlined her business and decided this is what works best for her and her business.

2. <u>More Personal.</u> Every doctor (or clinic) is now in direct competition with every other doctor (or clinic) in your area. The ones who learn to make personal connections will create bonds of trust and credibility with their patients. When we connect personally, the cost is only part of the decision-making process. When we connect personally and feel seen, heard, and understood, malpractice suits will drop radically, too! Win–Win–Win.

3. <u>More Fulfillment.</u> If you ask any doctor why they decided to go into medicine, undoubtedly it was to help others and make a difference. When they can spend more personal time with their patients, they'll be less likely to burn out or suffer from depression related to work and will be more fulfilled. (Remember our problem today health care trends from Chapter 2?)

What about the price for the visit?

1. 100% transparent, upfront pricing. (How refreshing would THAT be?!)
2. Flat, easy, cash-fee for service payment, just like many, many, many other businesses (Why should health care be any different?)
3. No insurance. No surprise bill months later. (Yay!)

So, what about the pharmacy?

1. Just like the doctor, this is YOUR choice. You're responsible for doing your own research, just like any other product or service you're considering.
2. Affordable cash prices
3. Pharmacists who get to know you, your lifestyle, and your overall health can also partner with you to achieve

    optimal health, whether it's lowering blood pressure, balancing your hormones, losing weight, or preparing for a special athletic event.

4. Did you notice how the pharmacist didn't recommend seeing an orthopedic surgeon, knowing full well that would involve an MRI and possible surgery with a scope, just to look around and see what's going on?

Okay, so yes, that was a basic everyday example, but you get the idea.

The point is that in a free market, the patient would decide and not the insurance company…. Now *that's* empowering!

Control.
Choices.
Freedom.

What if you require something a bit more major?

I'd like to share with you my wife Janet's story…

My wife has a history of colon cancer in her family. She started getting colonoscopies (unlike when recommended at 50) when she was 40.

Her second colonoscopy was due about the time we were going to switch from traditional health insurance to a wonderful alternative (more in the next chapter!).

With our traditional health insurance, right after the Affordable Care Act had been passed, our insurance premiums were over $1500 per month for our entire family.

We figured we'd have her get this procedure done before we cancelled the insurance because under the Affordable Care Act, preventative medicine is covered. Colonoscopy is considered preventive, so it's covered.

Janet received absolutely horrible service in the public hospital. She was supposed to start early in the morning, at seven or eight, but instead they keep putting her off until like 5 o'clock that night.

They said, "Well, you're going to have to come back tomorrow."

Janet said, "No. I'm not coming back tomorrow. I've already done all of the prep. I want to get my procedure done."

So, they did work her in. It's a good thing that she's an educated consumer who says, "Look, you're not going to treat me that way."

So, she gets the procedure done and we get the bill. Of course, they had no idea what it was going to cost because they don't know those kinds of things until afterwards. In a transparent system, they would know the price, just like when you go to the grocery store or get your oil changed in your car. They know the price right away.

So, after the surgery, we get her bill.

The bill was $5000. And it was covered, all right!

We only owed $3000!

But oh yeah, "It was covered!" Great! I'm so glad that we had the Affordable Care Act insurance, so my wife's procedure was covered. We only had to pay $3000!

Fast forward, five short years later... 2018...

We are no longer under any health insurance obligations, so we don't have to find preferred providers, etc. We are going to find the best provider at the best price.

Through some of our connections, we ask around and there's a clinic in Spokane (about 100 miles away) that specializes in these procedures, and they can get us in pretty quickly. So, despite the drive, we book a time.

The experience was amazing.

We checked in early morning at 6:30. I went outside to get my wallet, and by the time I came back in, they had taken her back to get started.

The waiting room was not full of a bunch of grouchy sick people like a public hospital. The receptionist informed me Janet had already been taken back.

I asked her about payment, and she informed me I was receiving the cash discount and it would be $1100. I gave her my debit card and it was done.

No surprise bills six months later (like so many nightmare stories!) or items not covered. They knew exactly what the cost would be: $1100(!).

The procedure actually was scheduled for 7 a.m. They called me back shortly after 7, letting me know she was done. The nurse and the doctor were very friendly, making sure Janet was comfortable and understood the procedure and the findings. We were back home by 9:45, even after a 1.5-hour drive.

To recap...

$1100 for the entire procedure, paid out of pocket.

$1100 paid for the doctor. It paid for the anesthesiologist. It paid for the radiology. All of that was covered. It was inclusive. None of these smoke and mirror bills where, later on, we get charged for something else. $1100. Amazing!

So, when we had traditional health insurance, they billed insurance $5000 and we had to pay $3000.

AND we had to pay $1500 per month in insurance premiums for something that basically wasn't covered anyway.

So, not only did we save $1900 out of pocket on this procedure, but we save $18,000 per year on insurance premiums. Now, our alternative program is about $135 per month for all four of us – so literally, we save $18,000 per year on insurance premiums AND we get better health care. To top it off, when we pay cash, we get better service, too!

$18,000 in family savings! Yowza! Talk about real money!

I did hear recently about a clinic in town close to the same distance that is offering the same procedure for $700. We will absolutely check into it.

I love the free market. When businesses compete, We Win.

So, what did we learn here?

1. YES, there's a better, higher quality, more affordable way to optimal health care.

2. We CAN educate and empower each other on how to proceed and thrive.

So, yes, these are just examples, but is it really just a pipe dream for everyone else?

No, I don't believe it is. I believe it's a very solid reality that not only is already happening for some (including our family) but can be the reality for So Many More.

So, how do we empower this to happen?

With the courage to not only imagine a better life for our families and communities, the belief that it can happen, and the willingness to take baby steps of action towards a better future.

It's time to learn about my 6-Step Solution…

CHAPTER 6 - SHAWN'S SOLUTION

"The best health insurance we have is not something we can buy. It is how we take care of ourselves."

— SHAWN NEEDHAM

Now more than ever, consumers need (and I believe want) to realize they can make a difference in their health by shifting their focus to clean eating, and healthy, active lifestyles.

It's time for a revolution.

A revolution for a major national mindset shift.

A shift of pro-health habits versus sick care. Of getting to the root, not masking symptoms.

Good health is truly the best medicine.

Now comes the challenge. The call to action.

This will create new entrepreneurial opportunities.

To educate all consumers.

To educate all health care providers.

To educate all health care institutions.

To join the movement and take a stand For Healthy Families and Communities everywhere.

So, how do we do this? It comes down to...

MY 6-STEP SOLUTION

1. Consumers Commit to Pro-Health
To manage chronic sickness with healthy lifestyle choices. I can't stress enough how pivotal this mindset and commitment is. Without the lens of proactive health versus sick care, you'll continue to struggle in most likely multiple areas of your life. The idea of getting to the root of the problem and solving versus masking symptoms is first an awareness of the concept, then follow through led by YOU, the consumer, (and not the health care industry as a whole) and then choosing if, who, and when to solicit others to help you achieve your goals. Yes, this includes funda-mental lifestyle changes for most (maintenance for the rest of us). Healthy, clean eating, regular physical exercise, quality sleep, and stress reduction are key. The commitment to own and control your own health is the first step towards optimal health.

2. Patients Take Back Their Power and Research Cash, Pay-Out-of-Pocket Options
When a medical provider is wanted, research the best cash, pay-

out-of-pocket option, just like we did for Janet's colonoscopy. Your choice. Lower out-of-pocket costs. Higher quality service. Happier consumers. Happier employees. Happier business owners.

When we demand to pay cash to the provider of our choice, we feel empowered and own the choice to not support the insurance system.

Also, commit to researching and leaving reviews for various providers so our fellow consumers can share great or challenging experiences with others – exactly like we already do for other services we use every day. Something like HealthGrades.com, but with a focus that includes cash services, quality of care, and of course, the customer experience!

3. Employers who pay for health insurance Offer Options to Return Pay to Employees via either a 401k, Health Savings Account (HSA) Contribution, or a Percentage of Both
My solution includes employers STOPPING the payment of health insurance for their employees. Instead of paying the premiums, either redirect the pay to employees or provide the option to deposit into a health savings or retirement savings account (Imagine an extra $1000+ per month).[1] The redirecting decision will be made by the employee, aided by a financial advisor, should they choose. It's not in the employee's best interest when employers dictate the care of their health, especially when it could lead to staying in a job for the sole purpose of keeping or having insurance! This is a form of slavery! It's comes down to Control. Choices. Freedom. As more and more healthy people opt out of the health insurance offered by their employer, it will drive their premiums up, so change must happen eventually. It's just not a sustainable, cost (or health!) effective system.

4. The Consumer (You) Pays the Bill

In the traditional health insurance model, preferred providers essentially have a monopoly on the market and do not have to work for a patient's business. They just sign on with the insurance company. The insurance company becomes the consumer since they pay the bill. This lessens the power the patient has with the provider of health care services, resulting in higher prices, frustrated patients, and poorer service.

Ultimately when the consumer pays the bill, the price decreases due to free market competition, and the quality of care increases dramatically. If you don't like the quality of service you receive, you can either work directly with the provider to resolve or take your business elsewhere, just like every other consumable we pay for.

5. Health Care Providers Adopt Cash Only, Consumer-Focused Businesses
Providers take a stand for the best health of a patient and say NO to insurance companies, thus adopting a cash only (non-insurance, non-third-party payment), patient-focused business. When consumers are footing the bill, they shop around. When they shop around, providers who adopt this free market mindset will adjust and thrive. Less effective health care providers – regarding customer service, knowledge, quality, price, and value – will not stay in business for long. This will also prevent many unnecessary procedures from being recommended and performed just because a third-party provider (insurance company) will pay for it.

In addition, providers will experience greater job satisfaction, happier employees, a more streamlined, efficient business, and happier patients.

6. Medical Cost Sharing Programs
I believe this is the future to addressing emergency and acute

health care needs and a big key towards optimal health for families and communities throughout the US.

So, what exactly are medical cost sharing programs?

Fantastic question!

The concept's inception dates back to the 1960s, when the Older Order Amish Church Fund started the "modern-era of burden-bearing."[2]

Medical cost sharing is a group of self-pay patients who agree about how they will share each other's medical costs in the case of an emergency or acute (like cancer) need.

Historically, medical cost sharing programs have been faith-based. Just like any membership, each has its own set of rules and limitations. See a full list linked in Resources.

It's estimated that over *1 Million people* are already members of a medical cost sharing plan nationwide! The concept is NOT new, very well established, and very well received by a majority of members, including my family.

In our modern era, non faith-based, overall optimal health-focused options are beginning to pop up – or one has in my research – and more are certain to follow, I predict! This is precisely the beauty and power of how the free market works, and I believe an important key to effective and affordable emergency and acute health care today and in the future!

For the concept of a medical cost sharing program, let's look at Knew Health. The first and only non faith-based option I found. Their bold tagline on their website reads, "Empowerment to Own your Health, your Way." Impressively, they even include health coaches as part of their provider network and monthly membership!

What a revolutionary concept! Not only do they proactively educate their members on a healthy lifestyle, they acknowledge and include the mindset shifts that are essential for long-term positive behavior changes!

Talk about the free market in action at its best. One hundred percent focused on the behavior changes that drive action for healthy long-term sustainable benefits!

So, yes, in some ways, a medical cost sharing program is similar to how we have been trained to view insurance. For example:

1. The consumer pays a monthly fee to become a member.
2. A majority of the membership fee goes into a "pool" used to pay qualified medical costs.
3. There are rules/limitations for what's covered and what you're required to pay, etc.
4. Each program has its own qualification standards.

So how are medical cost sharing programs different?

1. YOU, as the consumer are 100% in control. You decide which doctor, clinic, lab, MRI, x-ray, yes & even HEALTH COACH you'd like to see. Want to see a specialist WITHOUT seeing your primary care doctor first? Go for it! And many times, you may not need a specialist – or even a doctor. Want to outsource your lab tests? Your choice.
2. NO red tape when it comes to your health decisions. The entire process is MUCH simpler, as it should be.

This includes what the insurance companies call "prior authorizations" and is what they require before care can begin – wasting your time, your energy, and money.

3. NO ridiculous time off from work requirements for certain short procedures due to unnecessary waiting (e.g., Janet in the waiting room for the ENTIRE DAY at the hospital before her colonoscopy!).

4. Costs decrease as the need for doctors, clinics, and institutions to employ MULTIPLE staff for the sole purpose of dealing with the insurance companies and government (third-party payers) disappear, creating a simpler process and more efficient business model.

5. Happier, more in control, more fulfilled physicians! They set their own rates and decide how long to spend with a patient, creating a true trusted relationship, resulting in less burn out. After all, physicians have good hearts. Most decided to enter this field with the intention to truly help people, not to be insurance company brokers or dictated by the government's red tape policies that prohibit what's truly best for the patient. (Don't we see that as the doctor's job – to be a true partner?)

So, how does this work in the real world?

I'd like to share some incredible examples.

"WE FELT LIKE ACCESSORIES TO A CRIME"

Dr. Keith Smith, co-founder of The Surgery Center of Oklahoma, was interviewed by John Stossel, back in 2013.

I remember when this aired, it made a distinct impression on me. During the research for my book, we ran across the clip (the first part is fantastic, too!). What struck me was that Dr. Smith and his surgery center believe in price transparency and have waged war against price gouging, specifically aimed at the government. They've even gone so far as to post their pricing on their website!

For example, in the interview, Dr. Smith shares that the price of a surgery performed by the SAME doctor at the local hospital was $33,505, and at the surgery center it was only $5,885! The surgeon is an independent contractor with the surgery center.

Why the astronomical price difference? Price gouging by the hospital (because the government programs will pay. Remember the "free food" analogy by Dinesh D'Souza in Chapter 2?!) and a focus on efficiencies by the surgery center. After all, they're part of the free market system – in business to actually help people, provide high quality care, make a profit, AND provide top-shelf customer experiences. Wow! What an enormous difference!

I was so impressed with Dr. Smith's pioneering leadership in this area that I reached out to him to have a conversation. See the full version linked in Resources. Here are a few of my favorite takeaways:

- Prior to co-founding The Surgery Center of Oklahoma as an anesthesiologist, Dr. Smith felt boxed in by the hospitals (who were paying less and less) and the government (who reimbursed less and less). He said, "*We (doctors and staff) felt like accessories to a crime.*" For his last cardiac anesthesia he provided, he was paid $285 for a six-hour procedure. For his last knee replacement, he was paid a shocking $78 from Medicare! He saw how much the total charges were from the hospital and so was privy to the price gouging going on in the system, *firsthand*. He wanted to be in a position to act as a true advocate for the patients – and boy has he ever!

- One of Dr. Smith's first patients at The Surgery Center of Oklahoma (SCofOk) over 20 years ago was from Canada. Because of their health care system, a lady was in a _three-year waiting line_ for a hysterectomy (apparently this is common!). She was tired of getting transfusions due to her dysfunctional, painful uterine bleeding. She did some research and found their price online of $8,000, which covered the surgeon, anesthesia, the facility, pathology, and an overnight stay to make sure she was doing well before traveling home. Flat-Rate, No-Surprise Fee. High quality. Superior Customer Experience. Scheduled in a reasonable time! Wow!

- A patient from Georgia who needed a urologic procedure had been quoted _$40,000_ by a local "non-profit" hospital. The same procedure was listed on the SCofOk's site for $3,600! They let their surgeon know they decided to go to the SCofOk. The surgeon took the pricing printout, went to chat with the hospital administrator, and said, *"Look, I'm going to lose another patient to these guys if we don't do something."* The hospital agreed to do the surgery for $4,000. The SCofOk got a call from this patient and said, *"You realize, you saved me $36,000 and you didn't even perform the procedure!"* (THIS is how free market competition works to YOUR advantage! Incredible!)

"I DON'T HAVE INSURANCE. I HAVE SOMETHING BETTER!"

Many years ago, my son, Shawn Michael, broke his wrist on Mission Ridge while snowboarding, so we didn't have many options when seeking health care.

They splinted his wrist at the mountain. There was a volunteer nurse there who was super helpful and nice.

We chose to seek further health care in the nearby town. We knew full well that "Do you have insurance?" would be the first question they asked, (That shouldn't be the first thing they ask but it is, and it was), so to just get it out of the way, I told them I don't have insurance. I have something better.

I'm going to pay you today. And you're not going to have to dot any Is or cross any Ts. You're going to get paid today.

She proceeded to give me information to fill out paperwork to qualify for Medicaid or DSHS – basically welfare.

I refused and told her I'm going to pay them today. I asked for their cash discount and she told me they do not offer that.

They said, "Well, we don't know what the charges will be today because it depends on how the doctor codes it."

Which is silly to me. I can't imagine.

We know what the charges are going to be for a car repair or buying a new car.

We know what the charges are going to be for groceries.

And a car is definitely more complicated than a broken wrist, and yet we don't walk out of there without paying the bill. They know what it's even going to be with all the bells and whistles added. It's so ridiculous to think – what a poor business model traditional health care has – that they don't know what the price is going to be before you walk out the door.

Now that's a typical health care entity today that bills insurance.

So, anyway, we got x-rays, re-splinted up, and confirmed that yup, it's broken.

The doctor said he's going to need surgery and they're going to have to put a pin in it. We left. That was Sunday.

Monday, I called Samaritan Ministries (link found in Resources), our medical cost sharing replacement for health insurance at the time. I asked them if they worked with any doctors in our area that specialized in cash services. They referred me to someone in Tri Cities.

By the way, when I called Samaritan Ministries, I didn't have to sit on hold for 45 minutes to an hour, like you would for an insurance company. I talked to someone relatively quickly and the first thing they asked was, "Is your son okay?" So, I actually got somebody that cared!

I live out in a rural area, so Tri Cities was the closest place. One hundred miles away. I called them when they opened up that morning. They were able to get us in the same day. I know from working with insurance companies before that being seen so soon wouldn't be the case.

Anyway, we go down to Tri Cities to have the hand specialist look at my son's wrist.

Upon arriving, I asked them if they offer any cash discounts?

Yes, normally to see a physician it's $300.
With the cash discount, we can do it for $112.

I'm thinking, "$112? That's very, very reasonable."

In Moses Lake, my hometown, it was going to be $300 to see the physi-
cian. $300 for an x-ray. And an extra $300 to read the x-ray. So a $900
fee for all that!

So, the orthopedic guy sees my son and not the specialist because the
specialist was busy doing surgery. He said, yeah, he's probably going to
need surgery, but I'm going to run it through the hand specialist later to
see what he says.

Later on that day, we got a call. The hand specialist wanted to see Shawn
Michael and wanted to know if we could come back the next day, so we
said, "Absolutely." The assistant explained that it was going to be $112 to
see the physician, $59 for an x-ray including the reading. Which it
should.

But when I asked the other doctor's office why the reading fees were not
included in the visit and why it was $300, they said, "Well, that's what
insurance pays."

Well, I don't have insurance. Charge me what it really costs. What it
really should cost, not some smoke and mirrors insurance price.

Anyway, we went back the next day. The physician said, "Well, he does
need surgery, but we don't need to cut him open. And we don't need to put
a pin in. We'll just reposition it under x-ray and recast it. He's only 14
years old. He should heal and continue to grow and should be just fine."
And that's what they did. The normal surgery fee was $2200. They gave
us their cash fee of $700 if I paid that day. Of course, I did!

They knew the price. There was no smoke and mirrors about it. There was full transparency. They knew what the price was. I paid them. And we were good to go.

That same surgery – although it was a challenge to get real numbers – but locally, with the doctor, hospital, and all of it, would have been about $10,000. Of course, he was also going to have a pin put in him. Why were they going to put a pin in him? Well, because they make more money that way, that's why.

That pin could have caused lots of complications down the road.

Not only did my son get better service, but the price was better because we looked elsewhere with our pocketbook instead of letting the government insurance or health insurance company, which we didn't have, tell us where to go.

We decided where to go, and it was a perfect way to save a lot of money and get better service. It was well worth the 100-mile drive!

That's how the free market works.

Control.
Choices.
Freedom.

CREATING A NEW CULTURE?

To dive a bit deeper, I had the privilege of interviewing James Maskell, co-founder of KnewHealth.com. James grew up in the UK, moved to the US, and in 2013 had a daughter. As an independent contractor, he was shocked to see how expensive health insurance was in the U.S., so he started looking into other options.

James found Christian Healthcare Ministries (link found in Resources), loving the concept of a community taking the medical cost risk versus the insurance companies. He joined, paying around $500 (at the time) per month versus the $1500 he would have paid for his family for health insurance.

James has a background in Integrative and Functional Medicine, which focuses on getting to the root of medical challenges versus just masking symptoms (like when drugs are prescribed) as well as putting the patient in the driver's seat versus a doctor.

James' vision was to build a cost sharing community that wasn't based on religion but on the idea of **health creation** – a system that both keeps people healthy **and** controls health care costs. (Wow, right?!)

Once the individual mandate from the Affordable Care Act went away, the timing was right to bring his vision to life.

This is how Knew Health was born – a medical cost sharing program that's *Actually Transformative* for health care, with the principles that made the model successful in addition to providing proactive, personalized, and patient participatory health care (versus being told what to do).

The full gold-packed interview is linked in Resources. Here are my favorite highlights:

- Knew Health has been designed as a fantastic option to give those under 65 a chance to get out of our current health system altogether.

- In 2018, a Knew Health member's husband had appendicitis and needed an appendectomy. The surgery would have cost $132,000 if charged through insurance. Because they're part of the medical cost sharing program, the trained staff was able to negotiate the price for a lower cash rate of $12,000! As part of their Knew Health membership, they agreed to pay the first $1500. The family got on a payment plan for the $12,000 with the facility to solidify the "cash" rate. The community paid them back $10,500.

"The reason it's cheaper is because No One paid the $132,000. The reason it's so expensive is because no one knows how much it will cost. The system is so opaque. That's why we're doing something about it. You have to pay the lowest possible rates and that's cash."

- Lab costs are a huge way to save cash. You can go directly to the lab versus through the system. James gives the example of $17 versus $700! Same lab. Different charging system!

- The most exciting thing is seeing people work for decades in a job they hate just for health care (if they leave, they're going to have to pay the full insurance amount if through their employer, potentially $2,000) and realizing that If they join Knew Health (and potentially pay $600), they'll save their family $18,000 per year! As a result, they have an epiphany that maybe they could take a shot and have their own business, spend more time with their kids, family etc.

"Those are the most inspiring and life changing moments!"

The entire interview with James is fantastic! The most striking quote from him is this:

"If you look at the healthiest places around the world (the blue zones), they have the highest life expectancy and the lowest chronic diseases. Do they have epic hospitals down the road? No. They have healthy behaviors built into their culture! That's what we have to create... a new culture!"

A CLINIC THAT DOESN'T ACCEPT INSURANCE?

Tammy Nolan is an ARNP (advanced registered nurse practitioner) who is the owner of Choice Health & Wellness (link found in Resources) in Moses Lake, Washington. The clinic does not accept insurance. When asked about the benefits they've experienced with this way of doing business, here's what she shared:

- Daily her patients come to her for one thing, then ask about another while there. Instead of rescheduling (a.k.a. another charge like a typical insurance accepted clinic), they handle it on the same visit, if possible. Even minor procedures, too.

- She can choose to run a test that may not be part of the insurance or government's algorithm. Since patients pay cash, she can choose what's in the best interest of the patient without being dictated by insurance or government policies. "A good example is an MRI for a soft tissue injury. Most insurances require an X-ray first before they will authorize an MRI. This is super frustrating when an exam confirms it's not bone related. Paying cash for the MRI gets around that issue and saves (the patient) hundreds of dollars."

- "Sometimes patients come to me wanting cancer screenings. Some insurance and government policies would say it's 'not recommended or covered.' Just like any concern, we discuss the risks, benefits, specificity, and sensitivity. If they decide to go ahead, then we do it.

- In-depth blood tests for almost *half the price* of basic panels. Good examples are thyroid, lipids, and hormones.

- "The freedom for a patient to be in contact with me via person, email, video conference, or text. Without insurance, the cost of care is transparent. In my practice, I charge the same dollar amount no matter which method is preferred."

- Referring to the best specialist for the patient and not having to "stay in the system."

- "Overall lower cost of care because we've removed all 3rd party payers."

- Ability to utilize multiple treatments that may benefit the patient, but again doesn't fit the "algorithm."

- Ability to be truly integrated.

FAMILY'S COSTS DECREASE 45%!

We also had the pleasure of chatting with Business Development Manager Hillary Wilson, with Knew Health. She shared with us this fantastic success story.

Background: Rachel, 34, is a therapist. She and her family of four live in Michigan.

Situation: Rachel was notified that her monthly insurance

premium was going up to $1100 per month in January, for a policy with a $13,000 deductible!

Solution: With Knew Health, Rachel's medical cost sharing plan, her monthly fee went down by a whopping **45%**, to just $600 per month. That's an annual savings of $6,000! Plus, with this plan, their family's maximum potential outlay for unexpected illness and injury is just $7,500 instead of $13,000.

Rachel's Testimonial: "The fact that we paid more than our mortgage for our health insurance plan was extremely frustrating. That was the only plan we could barely afford (we had to work more to afford it). And we had a $13,000 deductible! We are self-employed, and the feeling that our options were so few was frustrating.

Not only are the cost savings a life-changer for our family, but now we get to be a part of a community and an organization that deeply cares about our health and is here to protect us and cover us when necessary."

CONTROL DIABETES WITH OVER-THE-COUNTER INSULIN?

Years ago, my nephew was diagnosed with Type 1 diabetes. My brother was very, very upset.

I told him that he can work through this and that Type 1 diabetics can live a long, prosperous life.

My brother is a very smart guy.

He did a lot of research on the subject to help my nephew conquer it.

I warned him that when his son was in the hospital, that there'll be a dietician that'll come in. The dietician will be overweight, as many dietitians in health care are, and she's going to tell him about eating carbohydrates (carbs) and how many carbs he has to eat.

Because that's how our health care system treats diabetics. We let them eat all the carbs they want to eat.

My brother asked, "Well, shouldn't you limit carbs with diabetes?"

"No, we just give them more insulin."

Basically, turn up the insulin pump. Great solution.

Anyway, he didn't want to fight with her.

At the time, he had traditional health insurance. He didn't really like the way everything had to be prior authorized. They would tell him what kind of doctor to go to, what kind of health care services he could access, how much they'd pay and wouldn't pay. And most things weren't covered anyway.

Because my brother really wanted to narrow down how food and exercise would affect his son's diabetes, he was checking his blood sugar many times a day.

The insurance company didn't want to automatically pay for blood glucose testing strips that many times a day, so they had to get pre-authorization, or they wouldn't cover them.

So finally, my brother had had enough. He went with the medical cost sharing company Christian Healthcare Ministries and started paying out of pocket for my nephew's diabetes.

My brother realized right away that he could do it for a lot less money.

The doctors wanted to prescribe all of these brand name, designer, long-acting, or fast-acting insulins as well as to put him on an insulin pump.

In reality, no diabetes can be controlled if diet and exercise isn't controlled.

So, he and his son worked together to help control his glucose to work towards optimal health.

And now, my nephew is on Humulin N and Humulin R insulin, which they purchase over the counter, without a prescription.

Most doctors don't suggest those because that's not what's promoted by the drug companies. It's not the latest and greatest even though they've worked for many, many, many, years.

When you control diabetes with over-the-counter insulin, not a prescription drug, it takes the insurance company out of it.

It takes the doctor out of it.

It takes those people out of the loop, and what they found is that the system is designed to keep you coming back regularly, whether or not you need to, because that's what insurance companies pay for.

So, the doctors and insurance companies are in this industry together. In reality, we as health care professionals should be educating patients that they don't need to go to the doctor as or very often, so long as they take care of themselves.

So now, my brother saves lots of money on testing strips for his son. He gets them at Walmart, very inexpensively, and pays a cash price.

The same thing with his insulin. Without the time, effort, and requirement for a doctor's prescription, they save a lot of money for the whole health care system and receive the best possible service.

In fact, my nephew treats his diabetes for less than $200 per month, which includes insulin, syringes, and testing supplies!

In working directly with my nephew, my brother confirmed that diabetes is in fact controlled best by diet and exercise and not expensive, fancy drugs.

Another story of the free market at work.

STILL SKEPTICAL? LET'S TAKE ANOTHER ANGLE…

I get it.

If the world of experiencing the free market in health care work - and that YOU can indeed affect change - isn't the one you currently live in, this may still seem a bit far fetched to you.

Let's take a step back and highlight some other real-life examples in other areas where this is precisely what happened:

1. Organic

In my full interview with James Maskell, founder of Knew Health, he discusses how it wasn't that long ago that eating organic foods was a very foreign concept. It took a while for people to get on board. Once they did their own research, they discovered the amazing health benefits and started to demand organic foods in their local grocery stores.

You Vote With Your Dollars

Where *You* spend money is where businesses looking to profit from what you demand (a GREAT thing!) will shift their growth focus.

As a result of YOU voting with your dollars, today, you can walk into your local Costco or grocery store and see for yourself how the organic sections have grown substantially in recent years.

THIS is the free market at work and how YOU make a difference.

2. Cosmetic Surgery
In 2007, a study conducted by Devon Herrick and John Goodman found:

> *From 1992 to 2005, a price index of common cosmetic surgery procedures rose only 22 percent, while the average increase for medical services was 77 percent; overall, prices for all goods increased 39 percent (see chart).*

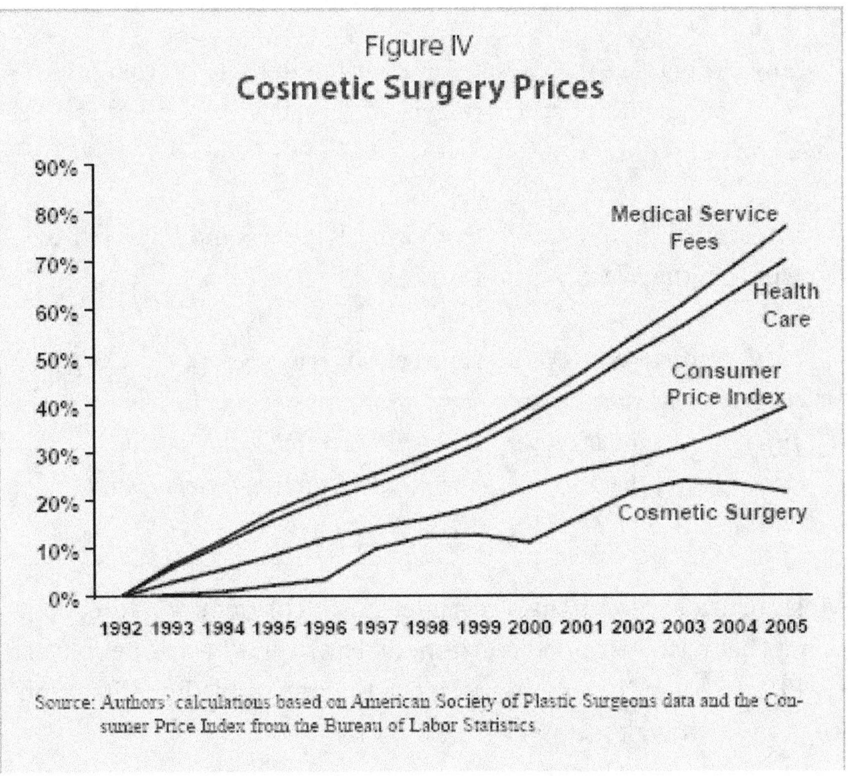

https://en.wikipedia.org/wiki/Health_insurance_in_the_United_States

In 2018, Americans spent $16.5 billion on cosmetic plastic surgery, according to the American Society of Plastic Surgeons.[3] Because these are 100% elective, they're not covered by insurance and are paid 100% out of pocket by the individuals.

This is a brilliant example of how despite technology advances and investments to obtain the latest and greatest by providers, the cost increases have been kept in check directly as a result of consumer demand and competition.

YES, the Free Market Works.

3. Lasik

If you wear glasses, the chances are very high that you're familiar with someone who's had Lasik eye surgery, have had it yourself, or have considered it.

In fact, according to a quote from eye surgeon Rand Paul, which appeared in the Washington Post:

> *Lasik surgery, when you want to get surgery to get rid of glasses, everybody asks the price.... The average consumer calls four different doctors. It's a very sophisticated laser, million-dollar laser, and yet the price has gone down by three-quarters over 15 years.*[4]

Most insurance companies consider Lasik cosmetic, so don't cover it, but that hasn't stopped consumers. Far from it! Most people are HAPPY to pay if they can experience the incredible benefits of no longer wearing glasses.

CONTROL. CHOICES. FREEDOM.

I love all of these examples. They represent just a sample of thousands and thousands of stories throughout our wonderful nation of how the free market system works when you have the right lens – the right mindset – realizing that we DO have choices and don't have to just blindly accept what the doctors and insurance companies tell us.

It is an accurate showcase of not only patient stories and consumer choices but of health care providers taking a direct stand for what's right.

What's right for YOU, the consumer and what's right for THEM as a business. THAT's the authentic American Way.

The result?

VERY happy, relieved, empowered, consumers AND health care providers. A wonderful and balanced win–win. Exactly how it's supposed to be!

The system we choose for the care of our health shouldn't **contribute** to the deterioration of our health due to high stress from simply dealing with this system, out-of-the-blue, unexpected medical bills, the uncertainty of being able to afford care, masking symptoms versus getting to the root of the problem, or the slavery of staying with a job just because of insurance. Right?! How many of us have experienced any of these in the past? Way too many!

The system WE choose for the care of our health should align with our values, be led *by US (not the U.S.)* and genuinely help on the road to optimal health so that we can live energetic, quality lives for the benefit of our families and communities nationwide.

Back when Janet and I started our pharmacy, we did so with the vision to create a better life for ourselves and our patients.

After our pivotal client story from Chapter 1 (and countless others) and seeing how our actions were out of alignment with our values, we made a decision to do something about it.

To Own Our Choices. To Take Action.

Our commitment to contribute in a positive way towards strong families and communities has not changed, and I was sick and tired of sitting on the sidelines, continuing to see families struggle because of a lack of education, knowing that there's a better way.

By…

- Choosing to be proactive with your health;
- Choosing to take back your power and research the best provider for your dollar;
- Employers choosing to give control back to employees with how dollars previously; intended for health insurance are spent;
- Choosing to pay directly for the care of your health;
- Health care providers choosing a cash-only, consumer-focused business; and
- Choosing a medical cost share program to cover emergency and acute care

… the idea of a better future for us all IS within our grasp. This is no longer a pipe dream. No longer an imagination story, but reality.

At the end of the day, it all comes down to:

Control.
Choices.
Freedom.

Control over the direct care of our health.
Control over how we spend our dollars.
Choices for who will help us on our optimal health journey.
Choices for if/how we'll spend our hard-earned dollars.
Freedom from insurance companies and the government telling us who we can and can't see.
Freedom from the government's red tape controlling what care we can and can't have (the government tells the insurance companies, too).
Freedom from the political pawn that is "Health Care" (a.k.a. Sick Care) used by both sides of the aisle.
Freedom to Control and Own Our Choices.

We've already proven in Chapter 3 the track record that the federal government has had, including the fact that looking to them to fix it is ***not the answer***.

The answer lies with YOU.

YOU are the Hero.

How?

Let's take a look...

CHAPTER 7 - YOU ARE THE HERO

> *"If there are no heroes to save you, then YOU be the hero"*
>
> — UNKNOWN

Whether you identify as a hard-working parent, educator, introvert, extrovert, athlete, professional, entertainer, advocate, creative, thought leader, or member of the health care industry, you may be thinking,

> *Okay, Shawn, I now understand your solution and believe it's possible for me and my family, but to really make a change for us all, how is this possible?*

> *I'm only one person. How can I make a difference? Where do I even begin?*

As an individual consumer, the steps to take have already been laid out. Here's a quick recap:

1. Commit to Pro-Health.
2. Take Back Your Power and Research Cash, Pay-Out-of-Pocket Options.
3. Employers that pay for health insurance, commit to returning dollars to your employees, letting them decide how to spend it (401(k), HSA, or an increase in income).
4. Just like other household budgeting, consumers budget and pay for the care of their health out of pocket.
5. Health care providers commit to adopting a cash-only, consumer-focused business (stop accepting insurance)
6. Research and apply for the best medical cost sharing program that fits your values and family. Think of this as your emergency and acute (like cancer) plan.

As a thought leader, entrepreneur, future entrepreneur, or philanthropist, in regards to my 6-Step Solution, let me ask you:

What further education is wanted
for consumers?

for employers?
for employees?
for individual doctors?
for clinics?
for pharmacies?
for other health care providers?
for hospitals?
for financial advisors?

What steps would it take to transition a clinic from accepting insurance to cash only?

What questions and decisions would be wanted?

When we ask the question, *"How can we solve (specific challenge)?"* our brains naturally will get to work to come up with ideas (why it's called brainstorming).

As thought leaders, philanthropists, entrepreneurs, and future entrepreneurs, we can then get to work on solving these challenges to create businesses that will create a balanced win–win. THIS is what makes our nation great. Our true American Spirit, genuinely wanting to help take care of each other, solve our challenges, and thrive as a country as a result.

When YOU get involved and take steps at a local, state, or national level, YOU become the HERO. The hero to the ones you help. The hero to your family. The hero to your community. The hero to your country.

There is no cap on the number of heroes. The time is right for as many as possible who are compelled to step up, solve problems, take action, and become heroes.

In fact, it's already happening, every day, all around us.

THE DPC EXAMPLE

Have you heard of Direct Primary Care? It's all over the news, Congress is talking about it, and thousands are taking advantage of this answer of doctors and clinics to opt OUT of the current "sick care" system that is tied to our national government and insurance companies.

This is just one of many solutions in place and is not for everybody, but it is absolutely wonderful for many Americans to help mitigate the upside or frequent-visitor risk.

Instead of paying a cash fee or having insurance pay directly for every visit, Direct Primary Care works on a membership basis. For a flat monthly fee, the member has direct access to their doctor, often in multiple ways – text, email, video, and of course phone! It often includes routine annual visits among other things.

I have first-hand knowledge of DPC clinics that save the cost and hassle of going to the ER in place of non life-threatening situations, because they have 24/7 access to the clinic. How incredible is that?!

THIS is exactly what I'm talking about! *True* innovation and ideas regarding what's possible for the proactive care of our health and solving the *REAL* challenges that consumers are demanding.

This is just the beginning folks.

As consumer demand evolves, those who are *actively listening* will benefit right alongside consumers by solving these challenges – in a true free market society!

Okay, so that should start the wheels turning at the local level, but…

WHAT CAN BE DONE AT THE STATE LEVEL?

States need to opt out of the Affordable Care Act and anything else related to the loss of control and choices to us as individuals so that the federal government does not dictate the health care market for us.

The state can make their own rules when it comes to health care, or even better yet, turn all control back to the People. We can best make our own decisions for ourselves.

Let the free market reign with competition so we, the People, can vote with our dollars.

WHAT CAN BE DONE AT THE FEDERAL LEVEL?

1. Talk to federal lawmakers requesting medical cost sharing fees to be tax deductible.

2. Talk to federal lawmakers requesting medical expenses to be tax deductible without a minimum.

Lofty, but HUGE ultimate goals would include...

3. *Demand that we repeal the Social Security Act.* Referring back to Chapter 3, this is what allowed Medicare and The Affordable Care Act to drive up medical costs, control, and lack of choices in the first place. The Supreme Court has already ruled the ACA as unconstitutional. Don't believe and appeal can really happen? The Volstead Act in the 18th Amendment (prohibition of alcohol) was repealed so we already have a precedent set! So, remember, Social Security is unconstitutional, and it brought with it Medicare and the ACA. Voice your opinions and remember to VOTE!

4. *Stand Aside. Get out of the Control Game. Let Free Markets Work.* At the end of the day, the federal government should not be involved in the care of our health. After all, they've already proven to be responsible for where we are today, so the decision stands that they are NOT the solution for the future of health vs sick care.

THE FUTURE IS YOURS

When I first made the decision to write this book and share the concept with others, the feedback was of course all over the place.

Incredibly supportive.

Are you sure?

It's about time.

Are you crazy?

How can I support you?

Etc…

The concept didn't stem from just one incident but from a very well documented, obvious trail that pointed directly to the undisputed fact the government **DID in fact ruin health care for us all**. I could no longer ignore the pull to educate others and to provide hope that there IS a better way.

We can't change the past. We can have our eyes wide open to it, learn from it, then commit to changing our future.

Ourselves.

I believe so very strongly that our current alarming health care trends, along with our ever-increasing pro-health environment, makes this the *perfect time* to embrace a real, actionable, 6-Step Solution.

We as Americans WANT this change. We CRAVE this change.

We're READY for this change. We're CHOOSING our commitment to this change. Despite the possibility of the lack of comfort we could experience in taking regular baby steps to MAKE this change. We KNOW this is right.

We know that continuing down our current, traditional path is not sustainable. Nor is burying our heads in the sand and pretending our challenges don't exist. We CAN however encourage, uplift, and support each other along our journeys to make this change for us personally.

In doing so, what kind of future could we achieve together?

My family and I, like countless others, are already LIVING this change.

I invite you, too, to do the same.

Control.
Choices.
Freedom.

The Future Is Yours.

Make It Count.

GIFT A FRIEND

SHARE THE VISION!

Know someone who should read this book? Now you can gift the book directly to them!

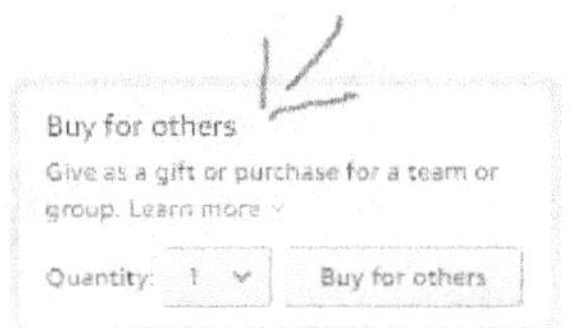

Just enter their email &
Share the inspiration!

HERE ~> http://mybook.to/Sickened_The_Book

#SickenedTheBook
#ThinkOutsideTheSystem
#OptimalHealthMatters
#ItsTime

WHAT VALUE DID YOU GAIN FROM THIS BOOK?

If you found value from this book, it would be deeply appreciated if you could leave a quick review on Amazon. This helps others find and benefit from the information.

Your specific feedback is much appreciated, and I would love to hear from you.

Leave a Review on Amazon
http://mybook.to/Sickened_The_Book

Thank you so much – You Rock!

#SickenedTheBook
#ThinkOutsideTheSystem
#OptimalHealthMatters
#ItsTime

Shawn would love to hear from and connect with you!

1. Request Shawn as a podcast or radio show guest
2. Inquire about Shawn speaking at your organization or event
3. Health Solutions with Shawn and Janet Needham / Live Show & Podcast

a. Live Stream via Shawn's Facebook page ~ https://www.facebook.com/profile.php?id=100006676787869
b. Live Stream via Moses Lake Professional Pharmacy's YouTube Channel ~ https://www.youtube.com/channel/UC4jgpI1BcHa-Hmpxw0bXuVDA
c. SoundCloud ~ https://soundcloud.com/healthsolutionsshawnjanet
d. iTunes ~ https://podcasts.apple.com/us/podcast/healthsolutionsshawnjanet/id1482969218
e. Spotify ~ https://open.spotify.com/show/2hcL38IQWGXMI-Ab4dSpGxT
f. Google Podcasts ~ search for Health Solutions with Shawn and Janet Needham with the app
g. iHeartRadio ~ https://www.iheart.com/podcast/269-healthsolutionsshawnjanet-61216231

4. Sickened The Book Facebook page!~ http://facebook.com/SickenedTheBook
5. Shawn's Instagram Page ~
https://www.instagram.com/health_solutions_shawn_needham/
6. Moses Lake Professional Pharmacy Facebook page ~
https://www.facebook.com/MosesLakeProfessionalPharmacy/

#SickenedTheBook
#ThinkOutsideTheSystem
#OptimalHealthMatters
#ItsTime

RESOURCE LINKS

* These resources are provided as a convenience only for the reader. This is in no way a direct endorsement of any product, service, or company. The reader is solely responsible for his / her own research when it comes to utilizing any of the below resources.

Chapter 2 - The Problem Today
Survey -> https://www.beckershospitalreview.com/payer-issues/
57-of-americans-have-been-surprised-by-a-medical-bill-most-
say-insurers-are-to-blame.html
YouTube video featuring Dinesh D'Souza -> https://
youtu.be/iYCSsaaRM94
Increased -> https://www.cdc.gov/nchs/data/
factsheets/factsheet_nhanes.pdf

Chapter 6 - Shawn's Solution
See a full list (health sharing ministries) -> https://en.wikipedia.
org/wiki/Health_care_sharing_ministry

Dr Keith's full John Stossel interview -> https://youtu.be/K4I44BcK39Y?t=505
Dr Keith's full interview with Shawn -> https://youtu.be/_SasEaMic08
Samaritan Ministries -> https://samaritanministries.org/
Knew Health -> https://knewhealth.com/
Christian Healthcare Ministries -> https://chministries.org/
James Maskell's full interview with Shawn -> https://youtu.be/DLGy3vFYE2M
Choice Health and Wellness -> http://www.choicehealthwellness.com/

#SickenedTheBook
#ThinkOutsideTheSystem
#OptimalHealthMatters
#ItsTime

ACKNOWLEDGMENTS

This project was 20 plus years in the making and 5 years in writing. I could not have completed this project without the support of some wonderful people.

My wife Janet of course who has been a partner in my life and business and family adventures for over 25 years. She is a great pharmacist, and awesome wife, and the best mother in the world.

I have to thank all the wonderful doctors and health care workers who supported me and my pharmacy over the last 20 plus years.

My patients who have given me the honor of trusting them with their health care.

My brother Shane, who has always motivated and competed with me to make things better.

My assistant, Crystal Kumpula, who without her this would never have been put in writing. She helped put my ideas to paper and develop and produce the final product.

So many others and too many to list.

Thank you to everyone who has helped with this project.

ABOUT SHAWN NEEDHAM, R.PH

I believe that there is a better way. The time is now to make a change. The movement towards natural, proactive health is already in motion. It's time to educate those around us that there IS a better way to achieve the best health of our lives... at an AFFORDABLE investment for us all. The best health insurance we have is not something we can get in a policy. The best health insurance we have is taking care of ourselves.

Are You Ready, too?

Help us share our story & spread hope for others by sharing our book with your audience.

We all have Choices. Alone we're islands. Together we're unstoppable.

#SickenedTheBook
#ThinkOutsideTheSystem
#OptimalHealthMatters
#ItsTime

~

Shawn and his wife Janet, (also a pharmacist) own Moses Lake Professional Pharmacy, is currently a Clinical Assistant Professor for the University of Washington School of Pharmacy, and teaches the Advanced Compounding Course. He has spoken on topics across the nation from hormone replacement, innovative pain therapies, and marketing a pharmacy. Shawn has a passion for helping patients achieve optimum health via hormone balancing and nutrition. He loves to spend time with family, snowboarding, hiking and mountain biking.

"Shawn Needham is an excellent speaker, who is engaging and holds the audience's attention. He has been presenting at our regional Medical Conferences in the Northwest for the past 10 years. The speaker reviews from the physicians attending, are always very positive and they find his lectures interesting and applicable. Shawn strives to always present current and relevant information that has increased our regional providers competence and performance."

— MELISSA RUSSO, DIRECTOR OF RUSSOCME.

WWW.RUSSOCME.COM

Presenter:

For: Continuing Medical Education @ Gritman Medical / Conference Center

Title: Treating & Preventing Disease with Hormone
Replacement Therapy

For: Columbia Basin Medical Conference
Topic: Hormone Replacement

Noteworthy:

Commissioner for Grant County Fire District Number 5
from 2010 - 2014

Served on the Grant County Public Hospital District One
Board of Commissioners from from 2001-2006

Clinical Assistant Professor for the University of Washington School of Pharmacy

Clinical Instructor for the Pharmacy 525 Advanced
Compounding Course

Moses Lake Professional Pharmacy is currently the training
site for the didactic portion of the Advanced Compounding
Course

Education:

Graduated from the University of Washington School of
Pharmacy in 1994

#SickenedTheBook
#ThinkOutsideTheSystem
#OptimalHealthMatters
#ItsTime

CHAPTER 2 - THE PROBLEM TODAY

1. https://imprimis.hillsdale.edu/short-history-american-medical-insurance/
2. https://en.wikipedia.org/wiki/Health_insurance_in_the_United_States
3. https://www.beckershospitalreview.com/finance/8-key-stats-on-medical-bills-healthcare-prices-and-out-of-pocket-spending.html
4. https://www.healthsystemtracker.org/chart-collection/recent-forecasted-trends-prescription-drug-spending/#item-start
5. https://katu.com/news/nation-world/fda-approves-new-breakthrough-cancer-drug-called-vitrakvi
6. https://www.washingtonpost.com/outlook/2018/11/26/why-prescription-drug-prices-have-skyrocketed/?noredirect=on&utm_term=.6f982958f154
7. https://www.beckershospitalreview.com/finance/8-key-stats-on-medical-bills-healthcare-prices-and-out-of-pocket-spending.html
8. https://www.pwc.com/us/en/industries/health-industries/library/behind-the-numbers.html
9. https://www.consumerreports.org/healthcare-costs/concierge-medical-care-pros-and-cons/
10. https://www.medscape.com/slideshow/2018-lifestyle-burnout-depression-6009235
11. https://www.ncbi.nlm.nih.gov/pmc/articles/PMC5587107/
12. https://www.ncbi.nlm.nih.gov/pmc/articles/PMC5587107/
13. https://www.cms.gov/Research-Statistics-Data-and-Systems/Statistics-Trends-and-Reports/NationalHealthExpendData/Downloads/highlights.pdf
14. https://milkeninstitute.org/publications/view/910
15. https://www.cdc.gov/nchs/data/factsheets/factsheet_nhanes.pdf
16. https://www.statnews.com/2018/05/31/chronic-diseases-taxing-health-care-economy/

CHAPTER 3 - LOOKING BACK TO MOVE FORWARD

1. https://en.wikipedia.org/wiki/Social_Security_(United_States)
2. https://en.wikipedia.org/wiki/Stabilization_Act_of_1942
3. https://en.wikipedia.org/wiki/Stabilization_Act_of_1942
4. https://en.wikipedia.org/wiki/Health_insurance_in_the_United_States
5. https://en.wikipedia.org/wiki/Ronald_Reagan_Speaks_Out_Against_Social-ized_Medicine#cite_note-nyt-1

6. https://en.wikipedia.org/wiki/Social_Security_Amendments_of_1965
7. https://mises.org/wire/how-government-regulations-made-healthcare-so-expensive
8. https://www.healthsystemtracker.org/chart-collection/recent-forecasted-trends-prescription-drug-spending/#item-start
9. http://www.aarp.org/content/dam/aarp/ppi/2016-12/trends-in-retail-prices-dec-2016.pdf
10. https://www.cms.gov/research-statistics-data-and-systems/statistics-trends-and-reports/nationalhealthexpenddata/nationalhealthaccountshistorical.html
11. https://www.cnbc.com/2018/12/17/insurer-hospital-stocks-plunge-after-obamacare-ruled-unconstitutional.html

CHAPTER 4 - WHAT HAPPENS IF WE DON'T MAKE DIFFERENT CHOICES?

1. https://www.bloomberg.com/news/articles/2015-05-13/in-russia-universal-health-care-is-for-all-who-can-afford-it
2. https://www.fraserinstitute.org/studies/waiting-your-turn-wait-times-for-health-care-in-canada-2018
3. http://www.nationalreview.com/article/432680/myth-cuban-health-care
4. http://www.therealcuba.com/?page_id=77
5. http://www.therealcuba.com/?page_id=77
6. https://havanatimes.org/?p=130072
7. https://havanatimes.org/?p=130072
8. https://www.washingtonexaminer.com/think-the-cuban-healthcare-system-is-ideal-no-cigar-not-even-close
9. http://www.nbcnews.com/id/16346039/ns/world_news-americas/t/report-spanish-surgeon-rushed-treat-castro/#.XKO2f5hKjIU
10. https://en.wikipedia.org/wiki/Social_Security_(United_States)#cite_note-SSA2018-9

CHAPTER 6 - SHAWN'S SOLUTION

1. https://www.ehealthinsurance.com/resources/affordable-care-act/much-health-insurance-cost-without-subsidy
2. https://mcsmedicalcostsharing.com/about-us
3. https://www.plasticsurgery.org/documents/News/Statistics/2018/plastic-surgery-statistics-full-report-2018.pdf
4. https://www.washingtonexaminer.com/rand-paul-lasik-surgery-shows-health-prices-fall-when-consumers-can-shop